The Guaranteed Timing Solution

Featuring the Perfect Timing Technique

by

Craig Opal

ISBN:
978-1-300-42687-5
© 2012 Lulu

Printed in the U.S.A.

Table of Contents

Please note: Since this book was written in 2004, some of the equipment described may no longer be available, but the principals are the same.

Forward

Here are some testimonials some are about the book and some are about the video. The book is more about the overall game including defense and coaching, while the video is only about hitting. Also please note: Since this book was written in 2004, some of the equipment described may no longer be available, but the principals are still the same naturally.

This first Testimonial is from a player who ordered the video, but had not received it yet and wanted some quick advice on the new technique, because he had two games coming up and didn't feel as confident as he wanted to. So I gave him the shortest version I could think of, but at the same time enough info to do it correctly. This has inspired me again to finally finish the book. Originally I had planned on the book first, but the video was just too tempting. No video can get into as much detail as a book ever could without taking 5 hours to view.

"I tried your techniques (without even seeing the video yet) and my hitting improved immediately! Wow...I almost hit it over the centerfielder's head, twice. He robbed me both times with some outstanding running catches, but I think I surprised them (and myself). I think I could have done your technique better than I did as well, because I don't think I swung through the ball as much as I should have....but your two paragraphs of info was great advice.

I'm definitely gonna keep practicing this and can't wait to actually get the video to really get into it.") -- *Sincerely, Dan Burke* http://www.nukleon.com

Dear Mr. Opal, I would like to say that this book is phenomenal. As soon as I got my book, I was so eager to start reading it. I have already read it twice and am starting to read it again, and I've only owned this book for a week.

Anyway, this book is very good for both beginner and advanced players. Not only did it talk more about the material from "The Guaranteed Hitting Solution" instructional video that you sell (which is also very good by the way), but it also talks about things like ball compression and core, and what type of bat is good to use in order to maximize for distance. This book is one of those "can't seem to put it down" books, with plenty of very useful instructions, very highly recommended if you are really serious in developing the perfect timing. Thanks so much. -- Sincerely, Orlando Morala Jr.

I don't know if you remember me, but I was the one who asked you questions after trying my first hitting instructions on rotational hitting at batspeed.com. Anyway, that video had some scientific stuff in it, which made some sense to me (why rotational hitting is better than linear). But it did not tell me things like timing, where and how to hit the ball. Thus, when I started playing again, I was definitely a better hitter (more power, since I was using a hitting mechanic, as opposed to just arms) but I had mixed results and never with lots of power.

Your video showed me things I have never heard of from other "instructional" videos. I have practiced on tees before, but nothing like what you teach. Mine broke that's why I ordered another tee, from you this time. But last year, using your instructions, I hit a ball so far; I thought I was going to break someone's front home window. Lucky for me the tree stopped it. I wasn't sure how far it went because there were no yard markers, but now I have to go to a bigger field to practice! -- Sincerely, Orlando Morala Jr.

I recently purchased the Anderson Techzilla and the instructional video from Opaline Sports, and here's is what it has done for me:

First let me say, I broke the top of my foot in a play at home, when some 210lb Construction worker barreled into my 130lb self and landed his fat butt on my foot. My batting has been in a slump all season (Normally I'm a .500 hitter, this season was a pitiful .333) even before I broke my foot. Lucky for me, while I was resting my foot, I stumbled on to Opaline just in time. I was able to "retrain" myself using Craig's instruction.

After watching the video, and trying it out in practice, and of course still working on it, I have improved my hitting over the last several games from .333 in 6 games to .750 in 4 games. It's no accident my hitting came alive again as I followed some of the simple techniques provided in the video.

I am not a "Power-hitter", I just don't have it But at the same time, anyone can hit a single. I bought the Anderson Techzilla with two things in mind. One, I knew I was not going to be able to realistically "flex" the bat much even after the proper break-in period. I'm a small guy with average bat speed, maybe even a bit below average due to my foot recently. But at the same time, my leagues play with a low compression ball. This meant I didn't want the bat to flex as much, which made the techzilla perfect. It has an absolutely huge sweet spot, and because the ball flexes and the bat doesn't with my swing, I get rock solid singles.

I want to recommend the instructional video to everyone, and either of the Anderson bats. You'll have to figure out which bat is right for you based on your hitting power, type of ball your league(s) use etc, but all in all, the Techzilla is the best "legal" bat I have ever picked up, period, and I have been playing for 13 years.

Thanks Craig for everything, and I look forward to hitting better and better as I practice your techniques. -- Sincerely, Chad from Yahoo!

Thanks' Craig, I watched your Video again today with a buddy, I love it, went out three times this week and practiced off a Tee, That's where it's at, like you said you can practice all three areas of the field, center and pull. From the first time using the Tee my head's on the ball and I'm smoking the ball. Couldn't hit one ball out the first few time's, but now with a blue rich's superior hit 4 out the last time and some hard line drive knucklers. All I can say is keep up the good preaching. Thanks' -- (Benny)

JUST WANTED TO EMAIL YOU TO TELL YOU YOUR VIDEO REALLY HELPED ME THIS SPRING SEASON,ONE HR WITH BASES LOADED, TWELVE TRIPLES AND ELEVEN DOUBLES AND A TON OF SINGLES AND A BATTING AVG. OF 700+ !!!!!!!! WHY? BECAUSE I TOOK YOUR ADVICE ON YOUR VIDEO AND STARTED TIMING OUT MY STEP AND SWING, ALSO ANOTHER GREAT PIECE OF ADVICE FROM YOUR WEBSITE WAS TO QUIT TRYING TO HIT THE HOME RUN AND WORK ON INCREASING MY BATTING AVG. THE MAJOR DIFFERENCE IS, I'M NOW A TEAM PLAYER INSTEAD OF A SELFISH PLAYER. JUST LIKE YOU SAID , 700 HITTERS WILL WIN MORE GAMES THEN A . 500 HITTER THAT HITS HOME RUNS!

-- Glen Matthews(another player happy to join the ranks of the 700+ hitters)

Your video has helped me quite a bit. I am still tinkering with my feet apart or feet together stance. But the timing technique is awesome. I hit .641 this season, BUT MORE IMPORTANTLY I was .750 with runners in scoring position! I am strictly a base hitter (never hit a home run in my life), but I led the team in RBI's this season. THANKS!

-- Mickey from Arkansas

Hi Craig, I purchased your video on 6/11/2003 and have been having amazing success ever since I started practicing the techniques you describe. I started using your technique in our spring games right away. Unfortunately I was not able to raise my average too much as the spring season was almost over. I ended that season at .512 which was up from the low .400's. The last few games of that season were however, quite unbelievable. In those last games I hit 6 home runs, drove in a bunch of RBI's (10 in one game), and most importantly, I was hitting the ball hard and consistently. Needless to say, my teammates and even the umpires have noticed. Some of them have been playing with me the whole time that I have been on the team and they are just dumbfounded (as am I) by my success. We are now 4 games into our summer season and the good news continues. I am batting .667 as of today and have 3 home runs. I have been hitting more doubles and triples than ever as well. Thanks for a great video. -- Brad Kirkpatrick (B division player, Washington)

"I would just like to say that your video is great- I just ordered it for my slow-pitch team and so far I am the only one who has had a chance to watch it. I had been having trouble hitting the sweet spot on my Rocket Tech, but after watching your video I have started using your timing technique, motherload technique, and two hand grip (which works great with the Rocket Tech's small knob) and I have been crushing the ball off the sweet spot all over the field. I can't wait to see what happens after the rest of my team watches it! Thanks Craig".-- Chad Beecroft

"Now, I'm not one to blow smoke up someone's rear, and I suppose you get a thousand of, "hey good video" e-mails. However, this is very different. I was absolutely ripping the frickin' cover off the ball. I've watched other videos without any success but yours has changed my hitting in a day. I'm a high 500, low 600 hitter, playing C/D ball. So I'm OK, but not great. I bat cleanup but usually hit the ball hard on the ground and hope to find a hole. I found myself topping a lot of balls. But today, everyone on my team was agreeing that they had never seen me hit balls any harder- EVER! THANK YOU!!"-- Dennis Williams (Another 500-600 hitter who is joining the ranks of the elite .700+ club)

"Craig, Thanks again for all of you hitting ideas!! I practiced your hitting method for about 10 days before fall ball started. I still cannot believe how hard I have been hitting the ball. EVERYONE is asking me how I am doing it. Hopefully they will be calling you and ordering you video!! Thanks again!"-- Dan Bono from New Hampshire

"I have been playing softball for 10 years. For the first five years I was always told I was a "homerun" hitter. I could hit 8 out of 10 pitches over a 330 foot fence. Six years ago I suffered a double shoulder injury in a bench press competition and have since recuperated but I lost my swing, My bat speed was slowed and my swing didn't feel natural so I became a placement hitter for a high Average. I've tried all kinds of gimmicks and hitting instructions in trying to find my stroke and it wasn't until this tape that I have gained back my missing bat. Although I haven't had the tape long and our season in Washington State hasn't started yet, I can already feel my bat speed has increased and my swing is starting to feel natural again. If the teams I play against want to stop me, they should put the fence in outer space because with Craigs tape the balls I hit are now in orbit! Thanks Craig!" "

-- Sincerely, James Marasco AKA Big Hurt

"Great stuff! I really like how Craig makes this simple to apply to anyone. This is not just another watch me hit it 400 ft, nor is it one of those "Your doing it all wrong, this is what I do" lessons. Craig points out some simple but valuable points that are missed by many! I have been playing slow-pitch softball for 20 years now and had seasons with averages over 800+ and 20+ HRs, and this video has shown me and my team some things to work on to improve as well as help us stay consistent... This one will work for anyone at any level! Great Stuff Craig! "

-- Jim "Pitbull" Peerbolte(Veteran All Star)

"Overwhelming Results" First of all, let me begin by saying, I am very grateful to the Lord Jesus Christ for giving me the ability at the age 55 to play a little boy's game. I also realize by natural law I have more years behind me than in front of me. But I'm not going to let that stop me from doing young things. Satchel Paige once said, "don't slow down they might be gaining on you."

Second, I want to thank Craig Opal for his teaching video on "timing" which is a key to a lot of things in this life not just in softball. One of biggest problem's we all have is timing, focus, and weight transfer. I don't care how old, young or strong you are if these elements are missing you will not be an effective hitter. While searching the internet I came across Craig Opal's video on "timing is everything."

I ordered the video and meanwhile I had purchased a batting tee because on his web site, he puts a lot emphasis on a batting tee for practice. Anytime you can pick up 10% here and 10% there it all adds up. From the things I learned from the video mixed with the things I already knew has made me a more confident hitter. I encourage anyone that's wants to improve themselves to get the video. "

--Rev. Sammy Lee

I've been using your timing technique for the last 4-5 weeks of the season, and I'm batting .687!!! Also, I've been using a variation (my version) of your 'mother-load' technique and I've been scalding the ball. In fact, the few times that I've not hit the ball hard is when I've lost my concentration and hit bad pitches. Thanks for everything! **-Rob P.**

I loved the hitting solution book I purchased from you. I have been hitting the ball a ton. Short and simple! -Mean Gene the hitting machine.

Well I had lots of fun for the first time this season at our double header last night! In May I started to play softball again after 15 years. Never very good, in my opinion, but the extra years made me bad. Anyways, bought the ebook and the video (I've always been a base hitter) and the timing technique made all the difference in the world!! Other than one 1 pop-fly out got on base every time about 9 at bats. Hit two infield homeruns (with people on base) and with bases loaded a double.-Don Stringham

Introduction

"Everybody back up, we have a good hitter and he hits it everywhere." If these are not the words you hear now, when you step into the batter's box, they will be soon. Total Confidence and perfect focus, coupled with a great system is an unstoppable combination when it comes to hitting. Welcome to the Guaranteed Hitting Solution featuring "The Perfect Timing Technique" for slow pitch softball.

We will also be discussing fast pitch and baseball timing as well, because it all is relevant and you will see how it all fits together in the end. Therefore, you baseball and fast pitch players can hang on for the ride, as we will discuss the stuff only the pros seem to know. Now it will be your turn.

This is New and it is different from many of your older books and videos out there now on the subject of hitting. One reason is the game has evolved fast and still is evolving even as I write this book. Two is I think they glossed over and in most cases completely missed the timing issue and its importance to all hitters. Oh sure your basic mechanics of hitting will always stay the same, but there are new and exciting ways of training and equipment that is revolutionizing the industry, especially just the last few years. Now The Guaranteed Hitting Solution, which I will now refer to as GHS for the remainder of the book, is and already has revolutionized many people's games by way of the video I came out with just a short time ago.

The only problem with any instructional video is the time factor and the video is already a whopping seventy minutes long. Of course, as these things usually go, I kept adding on and on and then realized this book is where I could store three or four hours of video information in as much detail, as it needs.

The GHS is not just a slogan I came up with; I believe it, live it and use it every day. The video and now the book starts where others leave off and it is a radically new concept may stun you in its simplicity. It has little to do with bat speed, which some believe is the only thing that matters to hitting. This new technique is extremely easy to learn and anyone can do it. It is about timing and all your mechanics revolve around this important issue that has been kept under wraps for too long. I have been fortunate enough to find an easy way to maximize this overlooked key to hitting that has always been there, but somehow missed. One day a few years back during a session of personal batting tee work, I stumbled upon this idea and then formulated a technique that forever changed my already successful hitting game.

The amazing thing I found was it was even better than I had hoped it would be. It actually compensated for times of non-focus and lack of eye contact and still allowed me to hit successfully.

I would never tell anyone to take his or her eye off the ball, but it is not possible to have perfect focus 100% of the time. Focus and eye contact is paramount, but lack of it happens occasionally even to the best of us. However, imagine if you lost eye contact and still were able to hit the ball anywhere you wanted and with power to boot. I have a story for you in a later chapter, which will show you how this is exactly what this technique does for you in those times of non-focus.

At first, I tried it for a year and my personal best before this was .690 for a season, which was not too shabby, but with the new technique, I hit .800 in three separate leagues ASA, USSSA and NSA. I knew immediately what I had found would be game changing to all who would try it.

The idea for this book came at the same time as the idea for the video did and initially, I wanted to have the book done first, but as things go, I realized a video may be a quicker venture and so now, I am finally doing what I wanted to do to begin with. This book will compliment the video perfectly, but also go into detail and also include new bonus sections you will find very helpful to all aspects of your game not just hitting.

The fact is most videos, while being potentially incredible teaching tools, for the most part only contain the basics, because of the time factor and keeping the viewer interested. In addition, most videos are completed and never improved upon. The GHS is updated with new information to keep you on the cutting edge. I am very exciting to be presenting this to you the player, coach, or both, because as the video has already changed the game for hundreds of players, now the book will change it again for thousands.

On the equipment front, things change on a daily basis. Low compression balls and hi-tech bats are now becoming the new battleground where technology is making such a huge difference, which they never were twenty years ago, at least to the extent they are today.

I will be addressing these new equipment issues along with the aspects of the game have been missed by books and videos over the years, so I will be plugging the holes which were overlooked, especially the timing aspect of hitting for softball both slow-pitch, fast-pitch along with baseball timing. I know this to be true because this was missing from my game for too many years and I found correct timing was in fact the one last key I was searching for in my hitting game to bring me to the final level.

All three of these sports while separate, have more in common than not and I have found the only difference is the speed and angle at which the ball is traveling from pitcher to batter. Add to this my new insights on all the other aspects of the game and you will find here a very new perspective from a different angle on a subject there is too little discussion about.

Correct timing in hitting will result in very high average hitting, when you know the speed at which the ball is traveling, especially in slow-pitch softball because for the most part the pitch stays at constant speed. Averages of .700, 800 and yes even .900 can be achieved by even the average player once all the keys are known.

Fast pitch softball .500 is not out of the reach of many players with the correct timing and finally baseball .300, .350 and 400 are the averages the elites in the game do accomplish. We will be looking at all of these timing issues to see how the pros do it so you can duplicate them.

I want to extend my thanks to you the players who have already made the video such a huge success. Many of you are on the testimonial page of my website www.softballhitting.info.

My hope is this game will be revolutionized one player at a time. It was many of you who gave me the ideas and feedback for additional material to keep all of us on the cutting edge. This is what the message board is for on the website. I welcome all feedback, so we can all stay on top of an ever changing and evolving sport to make it more enjoyable for all.

I am thankful for the last 25 years of experience with playing and coaching men's slow-pitch and girl's fast-pitch and baseball. It has been a great experience with much satisfaction to be involved with so many people. We together need to realize the importance of instruction as being the most important factor for playing the game the best you can.

Hi-tech equipment is great, but it will never be the key to whether or not you are the best hitter or player you can be. Knowledge is and always will be the biggest key to your success. Knowledge and information is worth far more than even an expensive bat. Knowledge is power. This is what makes a pro a pro. It is not only athletic ability, which sets the pros apart from the masses. Many great athletes out there never make the pros because of their lack of knowledge, mental focus and dedication to practice.

I have it all here for you. The knowledge you need, the tools you need to get good and I am dedicated to your success if you want to go further. I really do get satisfaction from helping others and watching and hearing about their improvement. This is the coach in me. I look forward to helping you as well.

If you want to get to the meat of what I am presenting and what this book all revolves around, then Chapter 3, "The Perfect Timing Technique" will tickle your fancy.

I also want to thank the late Ray Demarini for his video series, which made me into a .600 hitter many years ago, just as he said it would.

There are so many videos and books that have helped us all over the years improve our games that I really just want to say here, that you can learn a little something from all of them. The purpose of this book and my video is not to talk down about anything else that has ever been done, but simply to add to it and possibly plug a few holes or maybe connect the dots if you will to bring you a more complete picture.

Every coach and or instructor who has tried to add to the game in some way and bring something new to the table has affected the game because they all bring a different perspective. So while no one project can be a truly complete work, it still has value. If you learn just one new thing from this book and or my video, then it did what I hoped it would, elevate your game in some way.

Thanks for being a part of this ever-evolving group of players who want to improve their game. Your comments and suggestions are always welcome and I consider you to be not just what I hope to be a loyal customer, but a friend as well even if we never meet in person. And now onward and upward to what you bought this for.

Chapter 1: The Best Training Equipment

Even if you decide you will not be using training equipment in your practice, you need to read this chapter, because it is important to understand where I am coming from on box positioning and stance among some other things I will be laying the groundwork on for later chapters.

For as many different bats and gloves there are to choose from, there may be as many hitting contraptions and pieces of training equipment including electronic bat speed devices and such to add to your confusion of choices. Let us first assume they all work, because to one extent or another they do, but having said this you could spend thousands of dollars or one hundred and get the same results.

On the higher priced end of the spectrum, we have the pitching machines, which can be priced in the thousands, then electronic bat speed devices, swing-aways, bat-actions and the like which can be in the hundreds of dollars. Then on the lower end, we have batting tees, hit-aways and the like. I have used them all and yes, I do have a personal favorite, it is the old standby batting tee, so this is where I will be spending much of my time and discussion.

Let us consider first the batting tee, because in my opinion is it the most overlooked piece of training equipment, probably because it has been around so long and everyone wants to try the new thing.

Who needs a batting tee? I will submit to you, everyone needs to use a batting tee. However, not just the youth need to be taught the proper use, adults as well will perfect their hitting to best it can be with the continued use of this simple yet profound training tool.

The pros use batting tees every single day in practice. It is funny how the little ball thumpers start out with tee ball, then we as coaches and parents are somehow so eager for them to leave it behind and never used again. They are set aside in closets and garages never seen again.

If they are good enough for use by the pros then they are good enough for everyone else from age five to eighty-five. I use a tee every single day and have been for the last several years. My only regret is I did not use one sooner. I usually hit 75-100 balls everyday off the tee. I wish I could hit more. Some of you dedicated players may want to hit up to 200 a day, if you want to become the Tiger Woods of baseball or softball.

The tee by itself, helped propel my average from low .600's to high .600's in just one season. Not only is it useful and needed, it is also a lot of fun to use, especially on an open field with a fence. You can also hit the ball into the backstop or a net, but the ultimate is hitting in the open field so you can see where your hits are landing etc.

The tee can quickly become addicting when used properly and given a chance. It is like having a pitcher who always throws a strike and as you know, there is no such thing. Therefore, the biggest advantage when using a batting tee is you are always swinging at a strike, because you will set it up for a strike naturally. There is really only two important parts to the tee. The first is the base plate. The second is the stem. The base plate simply will keep the tee from tipping too much and thereby giving you a more stable platform to hit off. The stem is the part, which holds the ball. The wider and bigger the base plate the better the tee.

I now use one called the PSPT, which has a huge base plate of 22", which is virtually impossible to tip over and it adjusts to different parts of the hitting zone for hitting to all fields. If you do not have one with this adjustment, you can still easily move the tee to different parts of the hitting zone. It is also virtually indestructible made from tough high impact resins and rubbers.

You can buy cheap batting tees on the market for as little as $25.00. However, you get what you pay for and they will not last you beyond one season, or maybe even one practice session before splitting, but still a cheap one is better than not using one at all. If you can afford it get a good one will last you and it will quickly pay for itself. The set up of the tee is important. You do not just slap it on top of the plate and start hitting. There are optimum spots and placements you need to know about, so you can maximize your practice sessions. The cool thing is, where you position the tee in relation to home plate is exactly where you will be contacting the ball in the game. Do not underestimate the power of this important fact.

First, on the height for the tee, you need to realize most batting tees are made for baseball and fast pitch and no one has catered to us slow pitch softball players until now. PSPT and I just came out with the first batting tee for slowpitch which adjust 12" higher than any other tee on the market, so check it out on my website. It is called the PSPT and will last you a lifetime, or maybe even two lifetimes. You will hit more H.R.'s hitting higher pitch's because it is easier to hit the bottom half of the ball on a higher pitch.

Ok, let us start with hitting up the middle and then go from there. Assuming you are standing in the middle of the batters box. My definition of the middle is with ones leading foot (the one closest to the pitcher) approximately lined up with the front straight edge of the plate, not the back edge with the point. The illustration on the next page and in chapter four will show you the location I am referring.

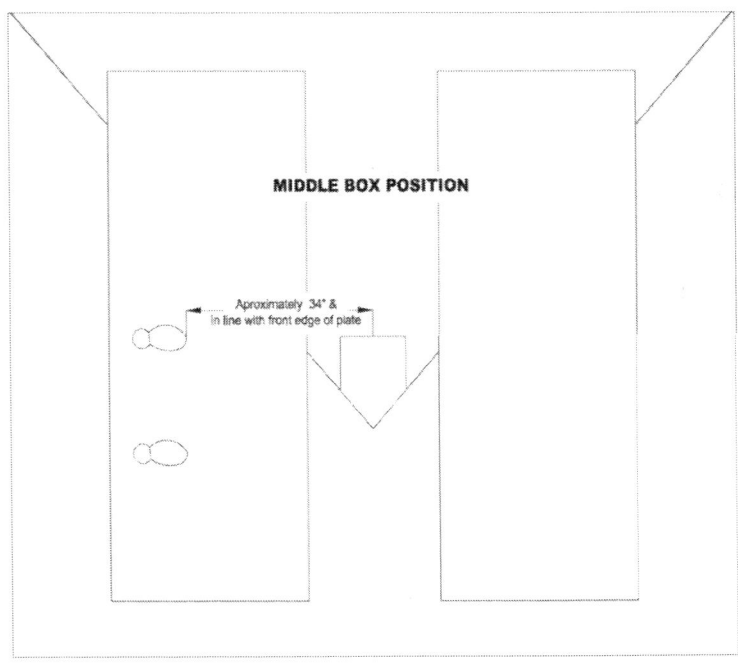

MIDDLE BOX POSITION

Aproximately 34" &
in line with front edge of plate

BASIC STANCE

We will first talk about a stance, which has both feet approximately shoulder width apart. Later we will discuss other stances you may want to employ.

Your distance from the plate I have noted should be approximately 36" or a full bat length (with the bat on the ground, not outstretched in your hands). This is where I like to stand, you may be different and reach has a lot to do with it. Just realize the positioning your body closer to the plate may not allow you full arm extension on certain pitches, so I like to be as far away as I can and with my arms out with full extension, I am still able to cover the outside of the plate too. This allows me to hit to all fields easier.

Please note the placement of the tee stem in these next figures is where the ball will be. Whenever I talk about the stem, the ball will always be included since they should be the same. This is where you will be contacting the ball for hitting to fields up the middle. Yes, you can move this up or back a few inches to your liking and note the different results of hit location after ball contact, but the following will be general rules. A few inches adjustment on stem placement will also result in slight differences in ball/field location after contact.

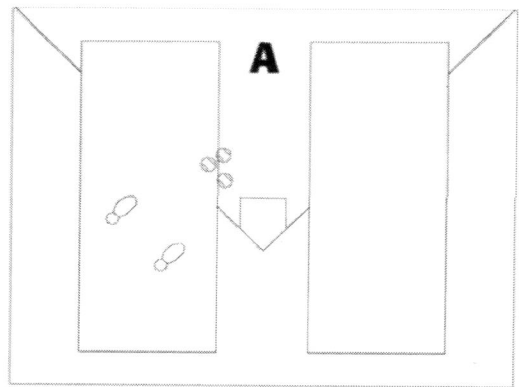

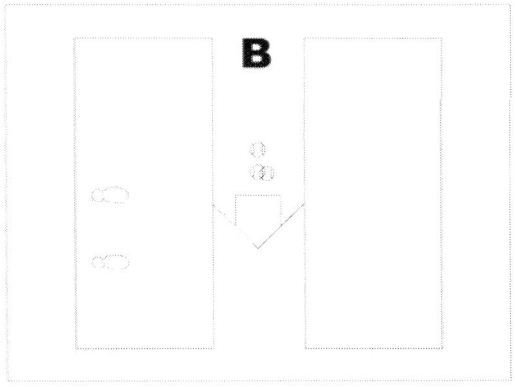

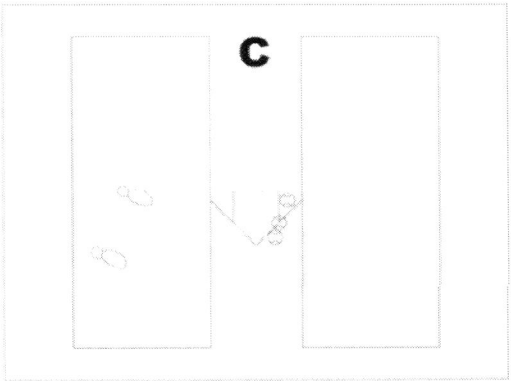

CONTACT POINTS

Next thing is to consider is, if you will be standing deep in the box (closer to the catcher and umpire), shallow in the box (closer to the pitcher) or in the middle. You need to know which spot will give you the results you seek.

I used to stand deep in the box in my younger years (and I am 42 years old at this writing). I have since changed my philosophy for the following reasons. I found myself swinging at far too many shallow pitches. This has always been a hard thing for me to control, but I normally can scald the low pitch if I try not to do too much with it. The problem with trying to hit a low pitch is if you drop your back shoulder and try to hit a homerun, your chances will not be good you will, because the homerun ball happens when you hit the bottom half of the ball. This is much harder to do on a low pitch. Also reaching too much will result in weak fly balls and grounders. If you want to hit the low pitch correctly, then only try and hit them through the infield holes and down the lines.

I have since found myself in the middle and even towards the front of the box now. There are many more advantages to being there. You allow yourself many more pitches to swing at and be successful. In addition, here is a little known tip about this placement: You are closer to the fence ha! If golf is a game of inches, then softball and baseball is a game of feet and sometimes inches too. Therefore, the difference between being deep or shallow in the box can be as much as two or three feet. Have you ever hit a ball off the fence? If you where two feet closer the ball might have been over instead!

Ok now we will discuss pitching machines. Great tools, but very expensive and they do not always throw strikes! However, if you are rich and have the space then knock yourself out. The batting cages are cheaper by the installment plan, but have the same inherent problems of not throwing strikes all the time along with not having enough room to complete your swing with full follow-thru.

Still it is better than nothing is but for the price of one season at the cage, you can buy a high quality-batting tee. Swinging at only strikes in practice is crucial in developing the perfect swing and correct muscle memory. Next is the 'Swingaway'. The Swingaway is a great tool, but again it is $400+ and expensive depending on whom you are. Many of the MLB teams use them and I was a dealer of the product for some time. It is my second favorite piece of training equipment after the tee. It consists of a backstop and a series of bungee cords and pulleys, which hold the ball in the strike zone and one can take hundreds of cuts in a short amount of time. This is its strong suit.

Its design and construction is solid and well thought out. The disadvantages are, it is big and bulky even though portable, in addition, one cannot tell where the ball traveled after contact. Still it has a great place in developing a level swing and muscle memory.

Next, we have the Solo Hitter. This is almost identical to the Swingaway except it is half the price. Now you do get what you pay for. The construction is not as elaborate or sturdy, but it will get the job done.

Next, we have the Bat Action trainer at around the same cost as a Solohitter. This revolves around a stationary axis after the ball is hit. You get the same muscle memory results with all of these training devices. You can hone your swing and get many cuts in a short amount of time and always be swinging at a strike.

Lastly, we have the hit-away. This inexpensive device attaches to a pole. You hit the ball and it wraps around the pole and then when it unwinds you can hit it again going the other direction. If this is all you can use then do so, but it will not be the answer to your hitting problems. The disadvantages are you have to be careful not to hit the pole with your expensive bat, not to mention it could actually cause injury. As with the other devices, this is the same in which you will not be able to tell where the ball traveled after contact.

This next device is not in the same category, but I thought I might make mention of it here. Any bat speed device which measures how fast your bat is traveling through the hitting zone. I suppose it has its place, but once you have found out how fast your bat speed is, then it is of little use and is expensive.

Chapter 2

Proper Mechanics for more Power and?

I think proper hitting mechanics should be listed in their order of importance to the hitter. Some are more important than others are. Some depend on others for their proper execution but we have all seen the player who had the ugliest swing you have ever seen hit a hard line drive base hit. How did they do it when their mechanics were so improper?

They had perfect focus, eye contact and good if not perfect timing. Therefore, without a doubt, these two mechanics take the prize as the most important. Eye contact, visualization and focus go hand in hand and are the single most important elements in all of hitting.

You cannot hit what you cannot see, with very rare exceptions and or a little luck. I have one funny example for you I will never forget. It was a nice sunny day and we were playing on a field where the sun was in everyone's eyes for the entire game while we were batting. It just happened to be that time of day and who ever designed the field did not put this into consideration. Well no one was hitting the ball because the sun was blinding us all. Both teams had no hits except for one person. Me. No I wasn't seeing the ball any better than anyone else, but it was the first year I was using my new perfect timing technique and because I was triggering on the balls release from the pitchers hand instead of trying to see the ball, I smoked line drives just as if I could see the ball perfectly.

We will be discussing this in more detail in the next chapter, but my timing along with good mechanics allowed me to guess at where the ball would be and the results were as if I could see the ball perfectly. I think the final score of the game was 1-0, which is almost unheard of in slow-pitch.

Anyway, this story aside, eye contact is still very important and I like the Ted Williams way of focusing on the ball in which he made the ball even smaller than it was by trying to focus on the stitching or mark on the ball before and during contact. This is intense focus. Another thing about this level of focus is you can try to hit certain spots on the ball such as the bottom half for backspin HR distance hits, or the top half for top spin base hits against which there is no defense.

Focus also does extend to other parts of the game, but it is most important in hitting. I like to pick the ball up immediately upon stepping into the batter box and not take them off the ball again until after its hit. This kind of focus allowed me to go on a 19 for 20 streak over five playoff games I will never forget.

The funny thing is I was 19 for 19 then blew it in my last at bat in the championship game. It was like someone almost bowling a 300 game. I had all of my teammates going nuts and saying things such as; he is awesome, can you believe it and on and on and I'm sure this contributed to my overblown sense of pride thinking I was in fact invincible.

Well I was not and I am not, nor will I ever be, but it is amazing what being in the zone and total focus can produce all by itself. Now the season was a different story. I think with that streak included I still only hit .650 or so and this was when I was 35 years old. It was before I was using the tee in practice and before I came up with the GHS. Also, just in case you were wondering, they were all line drive base hits to mainly the middle portion of the field, no cheap hits in that streak.

I also visualized all those hits before I hit them or in other words, I mentally thought out the hit before contact. The pitch was on its way and I said to myself this ball is going to center field and that is exactly where it went.

You need to do the same thing and depending on pitch location send it to the field in which the pitch will dictate. The inside pitch will be pulled and you need to tell yourself this when it is in mid flight; the outside pitch will go the opposite field etc. Do not overlook this mental part of the game that will make you or break you.

Proper timing, the trigger and the launch/step/stride all go hand in hand, but the launch itself is where you will be starting your whole body in motion to get maximum momentum and force at ball contact. Whether you employ a wide stance or feet close together or somewhere in between does not matter, the launch is where this trigger and timing process begins.

I also call this the start of "the motion to swing". Motion to swing is everything you do with your lower body before the hands come back with the bat to contact the ball.

The launch starts when you lift the front foot closest to the pitcher and either drive forward with it(the stride) to complete the weight transfer from the back foot to the front, or lifting up and back the front foot(the step) and leg before you come back the other way. I do the latter most of the time, but everyone is different in this regard.

A level swing is to be the goal at all times. Forget the extreme uppercut swing you may have learned or picked up by accident. The extreme uppercut is when you drop the back shoulder, lift the front shoulder and bend the back knee. Even in baseball, the extreme uppercut swing is no longer taught and the only times you may see the pros use a slight uppercut swing is with the ultra power hitters like Barry Bonds, Mark McGuire etc.

However, this is something they acquired over time not something they were taught. Ted Williams is a huge proponent of the slight uppercut swing, but there is quite a difference between slight and extreme. Still most MLB coaches teach the level swing now.

Slow-pitch softball is just a hair different. You never even need to employ a slight uppercut. Too many players get into golf swing mentality of dropping the rear shoulder, bending the back knee and or even chopping down on the ball.

I know you are not supposed to be dropping the back shoulder in golf either but the golf swing really is more of a chopping down motion. In addition, part of the reason this happens is so much is because many softball players do in fact play golf too. If you go out and play a round then play softball without correcting the swing, you will pop up an awful lot of softballs.

One way to remedy this is before you get into the game, is in the practice fungo circle or wherever you can swing the bat, practice accentuating more of a level swing or even downward swing. In the video, I mention a practicing a downward swing too but it is only to remedy the extreme uppercut. The rest of the time level is what to shoot for.

The ball in softball is higher when you are contacting it than in golf, which is on the ground where the shoulders and upper body will be trending downward. In softball, the shoulders and upper body are to be straight up while you go back and straight up when you come forward.

A true level swing is one where your upper body and lower body become one unit and move as one while keeping the shoulders level through the entire swing including follow thru. Also, avoid dropping the front shoulder and lunging forward to swing at too short of a pitch, as both will result in an uneven swing. Another reason a person drops the back shoulder is from starting the motion to swing too late after the balls release which results in trying to hurry the swing.

The weight transfer includes hip rotation and hence is where the term rotational swing was born. Weight transfer occurs the moment you lift the front foot. It shifts from being on both feet to the rear foot quickly. There are mainly two types of weight transfer and they both work.

One is linear where the batter simply strides or steps straight forward towards the ball creating momentum and force with minimal hip rotation. Alternatively, it can include very little or no stride at all, but simply a small step up and back down. This works especially well with high average hitting where power is not the main concern.

Nomar Garciaparra's swing and motion exemplifies this to a tee. Nomar doesn't take a big step back or big stride forward, he instead has a short compact weight transfer and his feet barely leave the ground, this takes much less time to complete. The other end of the spectrum is more of a pure power hitter like Manny Ramirez (can you tell I'm a Red sox fan) who takes a big step up and back with the leading foot, which at the same time accomplishes more accentuated weight transfer and hip rotation or rotational swing than does Nomar. This type of motion takes longer to complete and so he must start his motion to swing earlier, even before the pitch's release. If you have not seen the video yet, I will tell you I mimic Manny Ramirez more than Nomar.

When the hips rotate back, they must then come back the other way towards the ball to complete the weight transfer and the front lead foot will touch down softly as if you are on eggshells some would say. I do not think the latter is something one must think about and study, it just happens naturally. Some say you must hit off the balls of your feet and not the heels. Of course I agree with this, but again it is not something you need to think about unless you are unbalanced in your stance, which is what you would be if you are on your heels.

This touchdown of the front foot will in turn trigger the hands, which should be for the most part, stationary through this transfer. They will now come through the hitting zone to contact the ball and then complete the follow through. I have found simplifying the hitting process to be much more enjoyable and easier to accomplish than putting new terms on old mechanics and calling it something new, so while the above examples can be broken down further and have been by others, I don't see the need for it other than leading to more confusion. I subscribe to the K.I.S.S. (Keep it simple stupid) theory all the way.

Keeping the hands back and fairly close to the body until the proper time is another huge key to power hitting. The hands need to stay back as far as possible when driving with the legs. However, not only back, but close to the body as well. This is where true explosive power originates.

Arm extension does not mean you want to have your arms and hands out straight over the plate and out far from your body to start. In fact, the opposite is true. Good arm extension initially applies to the lead arm anyway and therefore is the only one to be concerned. The rear arm will be in the classic 'V' position until you explode on the ball, and then of course the rear arm will be in full extension upon ball contact.

Put another way, you do not need to start with arm extension; you want to end with it.

Hands low or approximately waist high are not a bad idea either, because even if you start with them head or shoulder height, they will eventually come down to the hitting position, which is waist high, so why waste energy and have extra movement, which is not really needed. In addition, hands high can cause one to chop down on the ball, which you really do not want to start doing on a regular basis.

Ball contact is important in many ways of course, but here we will discuss wrist roll and if it is even important to recognize. The fact is the wrists will roll over after ball contact as long as proper and full follow-thru is accomplished. This is not even something you need to be concerned with or thinking about because it happens naturally. Thank God, for some things, which happen naturally.

Relaxation during this whole process is very important. No need to grip the bat tight and stiffen the body, as a matter of fact my farthest hits have always been when the bat almost came out of my hands because of a loose grip. Deep breathing will help as well in the box and maybe even resting the bat on your shoulders instead of waving the bat all over the place, but whatever it takes to get relaxed in the box, then do it.

The standard grip which is used by most players is simply where the lead hand is down towards the knob usually touching it and the other hand butts up against it with both gripping the handle loosely in the fingers, not the palms.

If you want to or need to choke up (especially in fast pitch or baseball) this is personal preference. Choking up on the handle will give you more bat control and initial bat speed up to the ball, but less power will be generated for homerun distance.

You have to do what is comfortable for you. Some people hang the pinky finger off the end of the bat and some hang two for more leverage. I go a step further and use the double fist or some call it the overlap grip where my lead (bottom) hand cups the knob in the palm of my hand and my other hand simply rests on top of that hand. You can interlock one or two fingers for this or all of them, but I broke a finger so I no longer interlock any and I am super comfortable with this. One thing to realize when changing grips is it takes a while to feel comfortable with something new, so only try it in practice until you get comfortable. I think the double fist is great because it is a relaxed grip and it gives you more leverage and whipping action.

Stance is like grip, there are many and they all work, but I have found you primarily need to be balanced and comfortable. Crouch down or stand straight up?

Well most of the best batters I have ever seen stand straight up, but this again is personal preference. The only thing I do not like about a crouch is you are already starting at a potentially uneven position and this can easily turn into a dropping the back shoulder scenario.

If you are looking for something new, then I have one for you to try, but remember the stance is simply a launching pad and starting point for what you are going to do later on. The way you end is more important than how you start. I use all these stances with close to the same results, so to me stance is not the "be all end all". You may find the wide stance or one where the feet are more than shoulder width apart is a better stance for power, especially if you are going to take a big step or stride. It seems to accomplish more hip rotation, which I would compare to one jumping off a step rather than just stepping from level ground.

I also know some players who seem to rock back upon front foot launch to achieve weight transfer. If you can do this without dropping the back shoulder then do so.

On the other end of the spectrum, we have the feet close together or even touching stance. (Not to be confused with the closed stance where your front foot is closer to the plate than your back foot) I have heard some say this is not sound mechanics (the feet together stance). I disagree, because mechanics do not really start until you start some kind of movement. I do not necessarily recommend it for baseball or fast pitch players, but in slow-pitch, we have the time luxury, which baseball and fast pitch do not.

Also very young children may benefit from this if they do not understand weight transfer and are only swinging with their arms. Later on, their stance can be changed to a wider one after they realize the importance of leg and body movement.

I hit .800+ in three different leagues, in one season with my feet touching together so the mechanics of this seemed fine to me. I know everyone will not be comfortable with this but the reason I like this one so much especially for slow-pitch, is it virtually guarantees you will be striding towards the ball with some form of a step and weight transfer.

I have seen too many players who just stand there and swing either too late or swing weakly with arms only, this will help prevent this from happening. The only potential draw back would be if you were unbalanced, so to guard against this, make sure you are on the balls of your feet not the heels.

The stance and motion to swing as one complete motion can also be compared to a MLB pitchers rotation and motion. Look closely and see they are almost identical. Please note here and in other places in this book, I am not telling you or anyone there is only one way to achieve hitting excellence and you must do what I do. I am simply presenting you with what I know works and what I have seen work and done myself. There are many variations of stance, grip, and weight transfers etc., which can and do work.

Complete follow-thru is extremely important and may be in fact the one thing is keeping you back from becoming the distance hitter you have always wanted to be. Follow-thru has a lot to do with maximum bat speed and is maximized and developed more efficiently, when practicing with the batting tee.

I am talking about having the bat come around after ball contact and hitting you in the back just a touch. The top hand will release at some point, so there is no need to keep both hands on the bat. If you can accomplish full follow-thru and keep both hands on the bat, then do, but it is not required. This is the complete follow-thru you need to hit the ball as hard and as far as you can. I have seen many players shorten up their swing after ball contact and actually bring the bat back through the hitting zone the reverse direction. This is big no-no for maximum bat speed and follow-thru. Nevertheless, having said this I know some who are fine base hitters who do not have full follow through, so it really depends on what you are trying to do and accomplish.

Lastly, we have bat speed. It is last for several reasons. Oh I like bat speed don't get me wrong, but I would rather have average or even below average bat speed and hit for high average than blinding bat speed and hit .500. I know many players like this. Sure, it would be nice to have both, but some have more than others do and some of it is genetic.

Typically, bigger stronger people have more bat speed than a young girl or boy who is ten years old for obvious reasons. Bottom line on bat speed is you will achieve your maximum bat speed when you develop a sound swing with complete follow-thru. Yes, you can do things to increase your speed like using an end-loaded bat (discussed in a later chapter), using a lighter bat, choking up, achieving greater momentum through better weight transfer and hands close to the body. There are things one can do to improve speed, but bat speed by itself guarantees you nothing in the way of a hit. Bat speed is also more important in baseball and fast pitch, than it is in slow-pitch, for reasons we will discuss in later chapters.

Chapter 3

The Perfect Timing Technique and the Trigger

As earlier stated, correct timing is the missing link, which is missing in most books and videos concerning hitting. If this were not the case, I would have never written this book and done the video.

We will be breaking the entire swing down into many parts even though in the end it is all one motion. It is important to realize the differences between the 'baseball swing' for example and the 'slow-pitch' swing. Though I preach they are more similar than different and they are, you need to see how.

First, I want to use an example of someone who played a lot of baseball or even fast-pitch and they switch over to slow-pitch. Many of these players have a difficult time adjusting to the slow air flight of the pitch with good reason.

Their trigger or motion to start the swing is usually much too early for them for them to benefit fully from the weight transfer, which is needed for maximum power. Most of these players end up pulling the ball all the time and find it difficult to 'wait' on the ball. There are two easy remedies for this, which we will cover in detail.

We first need to know some things about the pitch such as speed and time it takes for the pitch to reach the plate after its release from the pitchers hand. We lucky slow-pitch softball players have a leg up on baseball and fast pitch because the pitch for the most part is a constant. How constant? How about two seconds on every pitch from pitch release to the plate.

This and this alone should send bells off for you ex-baseball players, but if it does not, then they will be ringing soon, as it did mine.

Imagine the averages, which would be attained in MLB baseball if they knew that every pitch was going to be the same speed every time. Would this make any difference in their hitting strategies and techniques? It definitely would. This is why you hear things such as he was sitting on a fastball or change-up or what have you. This simply means they have a special timing trigger for each pitch. The only problem for them is guessing what the pitcher is going to throw next. Since they know an 87 MPH fastball, which is the MLB average, takes two thirds of one second to reach the plate they can come up with a swing technique and trigger which will match two thirds of a second.

In fast pitch the average collegian and pro is throwing that underhand windmill pitch at around 60 MPH for a fastball. How long does this take to reach the plate? Approximately two thirds of one second, just like in baseball. The difference here is the mound is much closer to the batter, so in effect the 60 MPH fastball is more like 90MPH and more like MLB.

Do you think they know this? Yes they do, but again in fast-pitch, they are at the pitchers mercy not knowing what pitch is coming next, so they sit and wait for one pitch in which they have perfected the timing on. You can and will do the same thing, as I have done and do on every pitch. Ok, back to slow-pitch, this is my claim to fame and now yours. You are simply going to come up with a motion to swing which uses up the two seconds of air flight time. This is going to equal perfect timing on every pitch. You do not have to wonder what the next pitch is going to be like, because it will be the same as the previous. Sure, there are slight differences in pitch height, which will affect the timing a little, but not enough to fool you EVER. The only difference between a six-foot arc pitch and a twelve-foot is only tenths of a second. This is not enough to effect what I will be presenting you with because you will always be starting your motion to swing, at the same time every time.

Your new trigger to start your motion to swing for slow-pitch (if you are not already doing so); will be at the pitch release from the pitchers hand. Then you have a couple options. You can either start a two-second count in your head, or simply come up with a motion to swing which takes up two seconds of time as I have.

I can already hear some of you ex-baseball players saying but this is what I am doing now and it seems too early. Hold on. You are bringing your hands back through the zone much too soon. You need to take your short compact swing and expand it a bit, or separate it into two parts as I do. There should be two parts to the swing. 1. Weight transfer with the legs and hips, then the actual motion of swinging which is with the arms, bringing them thru the hitting zone to ball contact.

If you choose to keep your old swing and you can, you can still fit it into the two-second timing technique and this is the beauty of it, but your trigger will have too much later in the balls travel and the only problem with this is it is more unpredictable. This will result in lower averages unless you have perfect focus every single at bat, which if it was easy, everyone would be .900 hitters.

But here is the perfect or "two second timing technique", broken down further. I like to count like this: One Mississippi back, two Mississippi hit. I know it is simple. This is what makes it so doable. Do you know there are players and pros included who have never heard of or thought about how to apply this? In fact, when I developed this, I asked myself why I had never heard of this before.

Here is another benefit of the two-second timing technique you may have never thought of. It clears your mind of all the clutter you may be thinking when you get into the batter's box. How many times have you gotten in the box and thought; ok now last time I dropped my back shoulder and I did not follow thru correctly, so this time I have to compensate for , plus keep my eye on the ball, plus swing level, etc.

You see what I mean here. When you are doing a count in your head, you cannot be thinking about mechanics. In the box, you CANNOT think about anything but when to start your swing. Practice is the time when you should be perfecting mechanics, not in the game. Your mind filled with too many thoughts can mess you up easily. This is why you want to practice this so much. Therefore, when it is time to swing you do not think at all, but simply do what you just trained your muscles and mind to do.

Have you ever heard the phrase, be a patient hitter or let the first one go by? This almost makes my blood boil when I hear my teammates say this or anyone because it is backwards.

This may be more applicable in slow-pitch where wearing the pitcher down is not an option, but 50% of all first pitch's go for strikes. If the first pitch is a strike, you may never see another one. Add to this the possible loss of focus on subsequent pitches, because the reality is, you are never more focused and ready than on the very first pitch.

I say be an aggressive hitter, by starting and going through your entire motion to swing on every pitch at pitch release AND THIS IS KEY. If it is a ball, you will simply CHECK or STOP your motion to swing, just as they do in the majors on 90mph fastballs. If they can do it so should you in slow-pitch or fast-pitch. You want to start the body at pitch release(or before for faster speeds), because you will not know whether it will be a ball or strike until the last few feet, so if you are waiting too long to get things going you will have waited too long for maximum momentum, force and weight transfer for maximum bat speed. One problem with being patient is you just may forget to start your lower body and you will contact the ball too late in the hit zone and with no force at all. I used to do this all the time.

Some slow-pitch players prefer their trigger for motion to swing, to be half way into the pitch's travel. This may be when the ball is at the top of the arc. This is what I used to do too and it allowed me to hit around .650. Not bad but would you not rather hit .700, .800 or even .900?

This trigger is not as reliable nor consistent because you never know exactly when it is half way in flight, in addition, you are down to one-second reaction time, still enough to react, but more can go wrong and you will not have as much time to adjust. As we just discussed 2/3 of one second is what a 60 MPH pitch takes to reach the plate in fast pitch, so if you are not moving until half way, you are in essence now trying to hit a 60 MPH pitch. Even worse is you may wait until the ball is three quarters of the way to the plate, now you are in essence trying to hit a 90 MPH fastball or even faster. The fastest a human can bring the bat back from the ready or loaded position of hands back to contact the ball is around one half second. So for example, MLB players have the least reaction time of anyone and what they do to compensate for this is start their motion to swing before the pitch is released from the pitchers hand, if they don't they will be too late.

Therefore, consistency comes from starting your motion to swing the same time every time. The pros do this and so should you. They also start it the same time every time even when they do not know what pitch is going to be thrown next. I have found in slow-pitch the best time to start for maximum momentum, weight transfer, and consistency is at pitch release.

Remember this, which should be your new motto: Start the lower body early, and then the hands and arms with the bat will follow later at the proper time and simply check or stop your swing on balls.

Ok, let me illustrate further. On a six-foot arc, for example the pitch may be coming in a little faster than two seconds. It may be 1.9 seconds or so and a 12 or 15-foot arc could take 2.10 seconds or what have you. Still the two-second timing technique works perfectly because your brain will compensate for the slight differences automatically, because your lower body will be ready and engage the hands later to come through the zone.

This is the difference between being patient and being aggressive. Now having said this, I am not saying patience does not have any place in hitting because it does, but not at the beginning of the process, it is for the end and hitting to the opposite field only. This we will talk about in more detail in a later chapter. However, even when hitting to the opposite field, you should still start your motion to swing at pitch release because you will simply be waiting for the pitch to cross or approach the plate before you contact it.

I remember recently facing a pitcher with a very high arc of 12-15 feet; I still started my motion at pitch release. Then my weight and front foot came back and I simply hung in mid air a few tenths of a second longer than if it was a lower pitch and I contacted the ball on the back outside edge of the plate and hit it to the opposite field. I remember going eight for eight in that double header while most people could not hit him.

There is another way of looking at this technique and classifying it for you scientific type minds. This technique is one of total aggressiveness and constant movement. Not movement of the wrong things, such as the hands or head, but movement of the lower body, legs and hips. Jason Veritek, the Red sox catcher, is a great example of this type of aggressive hitting and one who I would not mind modeling myself after.

I doubt few would dispute the elite hitter he is becoming. The beauty of this timing technique is you are always going to be ready and in the hitting position, with maximum momentum and force and giving yourself plenty of time to muster the bat speed which until now, only the biggest hitters in the game could harness.

Now some people who try this, especially the players who have always swung with upper body only and players who switched from baseball with that short compact swing, may find themselves starting to develop what some would call a double hitch in their swing. This is the player bringing the hands forward too soon and not in concert with the legs which should have already started this process. So wait for the legs and front foot to tell the hands it is now ok to come forward and that hitch will disappear.

Again and you will see this emphasized throughout the book because it is so important; start the legs early to set yourself up for maximum weight transfer then bring the hands through the hitting zone with maximum force to contact.

You will have extreme confidence and know what to do on every pitch. You want to become like a robot which does exactly the same thing all of the time. The opposing team will now shudder every time you step into the batter's box.

Chapter 4

Hitting to all fields and contact points

Having the ability to hit to all fields, is an advantage the best players in the game all share. Hitting just to one field only, can be defended much easier and will cut down on your chances of success greatly. Keeping the other team guessing as to which field you will be hitting it to, is a formidable weapon all by itself. Add to it a little power and you will be one of the most feared hitters on your team and league.

Most high average hitters all share this trait and for the most part are the leadoff hitters or at least in the top 4 spots in the batting order and are the consummate MVP's year in and year out. For this, we will want to pull out the tee again. Really for everything I teach and do the tee is the perfect tool. This is where the hit-away and a few other contraptions come up short. Once you master the art of hitting off the tee, it will not take long for you to go and do it at the cages, then at team practice etc. Start and stay with the tee and you will amaze yourself on how quickly your game will improve. Contact points with the tee and pitch location should dictate which field you will be hitting to and nothing else. Contact points will change depending where you are positioned in the batter's box, location of the pitch etc., but you will not have to change your swing or stride at all.

The illustrations in this chapter will show where these contact points are. Let us now take the tee from the middle front edge of the plate, (which is where we last left it in chapter 3). We are now going to move it to the back outside edge of the plate, so the stem and ball are positioned on the back point before it turns in to make the roof-like shape in the very back.

It is from here you will be practicing your hitting down the opposite field line, (this is assuming you are standing in the middle of the batter's box). Note Fig. C on the next page for opposite field hitting.

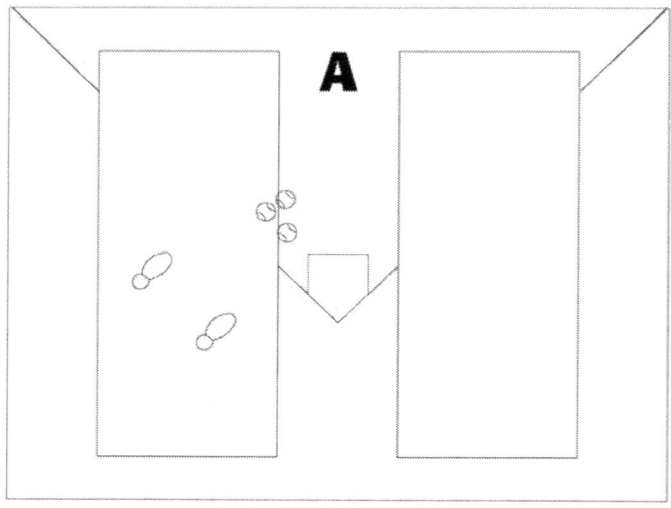

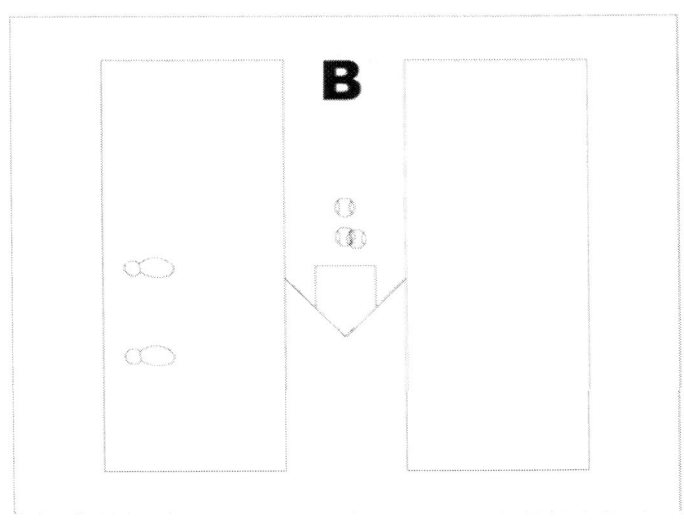

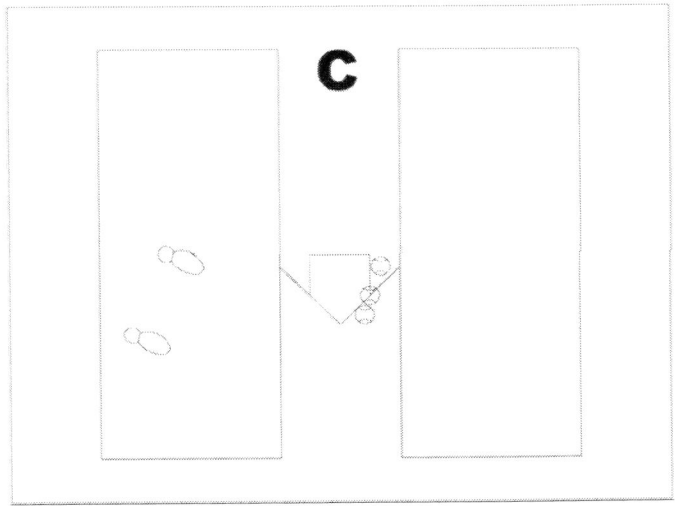

55

Also note in Fig A we have a bit of an open stance being portrayed there. This is not needed to hit an inside pitch, but some of you may tend to open up that way when pulling the ball. That is not a major problem, but do strive for more of a straight stride when possible for more power. In addition, Fig C shows a closed stance which is not needed to hit to the opposite field, but you may tend to open up that way when hitting the ball the other way. Again not a major problem but it is not needed.

If you are deeper in the box, then this contact point will change accordingly and be back even farther towards the back point but still on the outside edge. If you are very shallow toward the front and pitcher, this may change to the front outside edge of the plate. Remember you are duplicating where a pitch is going to be contacted in the game and why I love the tee so much.

For hitting to Right Center field (for a right-handed batter), and again in the middle of the box, move the stem to the front outside edge of the plate. See Fig.B for hitting up the middle. Position the tee right in the middle front edge or even 6-12" in front middle toward the pitcher's mound. To hit to Left Center put it out in front lined up with the inside edge of the plate but 12"-18" in front see fig A. For pull hitting down the line, I like to have the tee way out in front 24"-36" and lined up with the front edge or even inside more than this. Again, depending on your position in the box these contact points will vary. See the next few pages for batter's box positioning.

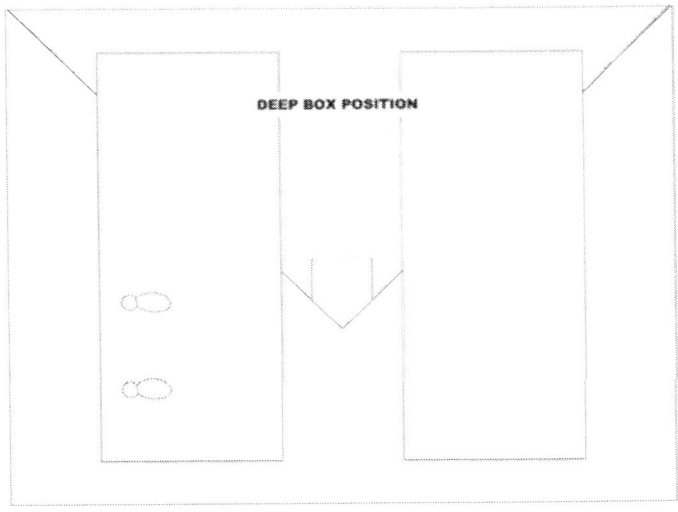

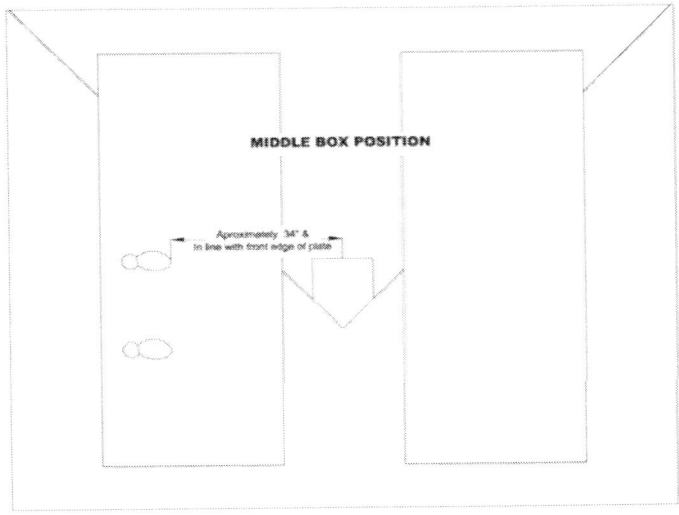

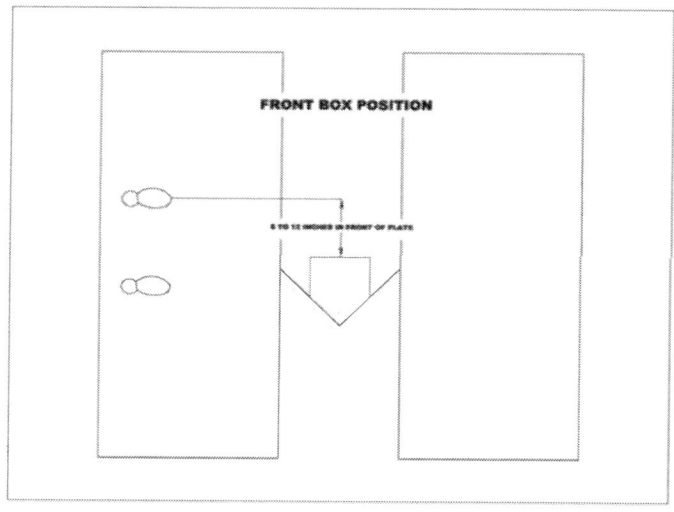

FRONT BOX POSITION

You will note on the front box position the front leading foot is 6"-12" in front of the plate before the stride is even started. This is good box position for HR hitters because you will be swinging at higher pitches. This is what you want to hit the bottom half of the ball.

The middle box position is good position for line drives with the occasional HR here and there. You should get a good mix of pitches to hit from here. Also note I have shown 34"-36" distance away from the plate so the pitcher cannot take the inside pitch away from me. This is where I like to stand you may be different.

The deep box position is OK, but you will have to be much more disciplined back there to guard against hitting the shallow pitch.

Now what you want to do is make sure your arms are fully extended at all contact points and you are striking the ball in the sweet spot of the bat. You will find as I have, this is accomplished easier when you are further away from the plate like a full bat length or 36" in actual distance. You want to give yourself plenty of room to step into the ball to hit it on the sweet spot and give it the ride of its life. One more clarification and this goes to arm extension, you do not want to be contacting the ball later in the balls flight than what I have just laid out here. Late contact results in pop flies and weak swings in general because of the arms not fully extended at ball contact.

Do this simple exercise and see where your contact point should always be. Standing with your front foot closest to the pitcher's mound and lined up on the front edge of the plate, stretch your leading arm at a 90-degree angle and straight out over the front edge of the plate. As you do this you will see that it should be stretching across the entire front edge of the plate. Your contact should never be past this towards the catcher (unless you are deeper in the box). If it is, you will be missing full arm extension and power. Therefore, your front leading shoulder should be the last barrier at which the ball NEVER GOES BEYOND. If you contact it in the middle of your body, you are missing full arm extension.

This is what I call hitting the ball out in front of you. Not out in the middle of your body but out towards and in front of your leading shoulder. Please note this next illustration, which is the most important position in all of hitting:

This position and location in relation to the ball is ALWAYS where you want to be hitting the ball. Note the ball is not at the bat yet but the body is fully engaged and ready to explode on the ball with maximum force. Everything is located behind the front shoulder. The arms are not yet fully extended, but they will be. Notice how he will be contacting the ball way out in front of his front foot. If that ball were just one more foot further in its flight and in the middle of his body, it would be much too late.

Other ways of describing it that I like is, either hitting the ball out on your front foot, or the bat and your lead arm will be contacting the ball and everything else will be behind these two. Shoulders head and elbows. Therefore, if the ball is allowed to pass the front leading shoulder you will not have the power you are striving for.

Moreover, this includes opposite field hitting. You still want everything behind the front shoulder even when hitting the opposite way. This is another huge key to power. Most all ball contact is too late in the ball flight, not too early.

Here is a saying that I just love. It sounds like another Yogi Berraism, and I think I made this one up. "Hit the ball before it gets there." I say it all the time and everyone looks at me as if I have two heads. (Sorry if you have two heads) How does one hit something that is not there yet? Here is what I mean. Do not wait for the ball to be on top of you before you contact it. Again, example of a player standing with their front foot lined up with the front edge of the plate or approximate middle of the box. They need to contact the ball just slightly before it reaches the plate, so hit it before it gets "there" is the plate in this example. The only exception to this would be opposite field hitting or if you are deep in the box.

Chapter 5:

Homeruns or base hits?

Ah the age old question. Do you go for one or the other or both? Well I will tell you what I do then you can decide for yourself what kind of hitter you want to be. We will also discuss how to hit more of each. Even though we already covered the perfect timing technique, we did not yet discuss the importance of differences in ball spin.

There is no doubt about it we all want to hit homeruns. We like the glory the prestige and the feeling of power and admiration we get from our peers. However, what percentages of homeruns actually end up helping a team to win a game or a tournament in slow-pitch? I am not talking about Major A's where the scores are 75 to 68 and the majority of the runs are over the fence.

99.9% of us do not play major A ball, so we can get real here I think. The majority of games won by a HR are slim and this is just the facts. The cool thing is anyone can get the game winning hit but not everyone can hit a game winning homerun. It is because of this alone in slow-pitch that I think you should go for base hits over homeruns. This will depend of course on who you are and we will find this out quite easily. Because the average team can easily string 10 or more base hits together in an inning to score six or seven runs, this is what you should try for. When is the last time you saw ten homeruns hit in a row?

Again, I know in the major A slow-pitch this happens, but I am talking about you and your team. Baseball and fast pitch is a much different thing and runs are at a premium at best. So in those venues the single homerun can win the game. I give you two scenario's where you are the coach and you have a player at second base, 2 outs, game tied, you are home team. A base hit scores the winning run.

Would you rather have your big power hitter coming up who hits around .500, but hits the ball 350-400ft, or would you rather have your leadoff type person who might hit .700+ mostly line drive singles to bat in this situation?

I think we all know whom the smart money is on in this instance and is why high average hitters, are more valuable to a team than power hitters are (in slow-pitch). Sorry you big ape, you are fun to watch when you are hitting a HR, but we really only keep you around for the intimidation factor. Most coaches would agree with this and I would stack a team of .700 hitters up against a power team any day and come away with the win nine out of ten times. Ok enough preaching. You are going to do what you are going to do and who am I to rain on your parade.

What I like to do, is get the homeruns out of my system in practice off the tee and then when it comes game time its high average hitting for me. I do it for many reasons. One is I am the coach so I try to set a good example. Two is I rarely see a good homerun pitch to hit anymore; too many people know me. You may be in the same boat.

Three is its just plain easier to get a base hit. Four is it actually does help the team more than an individual act of trying to hit a homerun. Nevertheless, on to what you want to know. Hitting homeruns is not as difficult as they may seem. I can hit one out of two swings on a good day over a 320 ft. fence and the way I do it is simply by hitting the bottom half of the ball to achieve backspin which will take it over the fence. Easier said than done perhaps, but there really is no other way to do it. The best way to practice hitting the HR is again off the tee for the following reasons.

You can really concentrate on the bottom half of the ball on the tee like nothing else. I would even encourage you to mark a spot on the ball whether it is a line or a dot below the half line or what have you. You can even take the ball, color half of it one color, and leave the other white to focus on hitting the different halves. This will make it easier to focus on this.

The feedback you get when hitting off the tee is like none other. You also want a level swing, full follow-thru and a relaxed grip to maximize your chances. The tee stem will be struck slightly and will move when you are hitting the bottom half correctly. If you hit the top half, the tee will not move at all. You can hit the ball as hard as you can, but if you hit the top half, it creates top spin that causes the ball to go over the infielder's heads and dive in front of the outfielders for a top spin line drive.

Therefore, your chances of hitting it over a deep fence are not good with this kind of spin. Of course, genetics does have a little to do with hitting homeruns too, but it is not everything. Also with the level swing, it is important to realize why it works better in slow-pitch than does an uppercut swing or a chopping down type of swing. It is because of the angle of the ball coming in from high to low, as opposed to baseball, which is coming in more level or even from low to high or low to level and the same in fast pitch.

This creates a scenario where is it much easier to create backspin especially with a level swing simply by contacting the ball straight on. The reason for this is it is easier to hit the bottom half of the ball with power on a higher pitch, which in slow-pitch is a pitch that many people see and send long. Even in baseball and fast pitch this is true and why pitchers try and keep the ball down and low to prevent the long ball.

Lastly, on this subject I will just say if you are doing everything right, and you have your level swing down and still can't hit a homerun, then it's time to accept who you are and strategize what kind of hitter you will become for the team and yourself. This is especially true if you cannot hit a homerun off the batting tee. If you cannot hit a homerun off a tee then you cannot hit a homerun. This is just the facts.

The following sounds like another something Yogi Berra would say, but homeruns happen when homerun hitters are up at the plate. Profound words indeed, but in the big scheme of things, know that 90% of all of us are not true HR hitters. Many of us hit them occasionally and is probably the best way to do it anyhow.

The sooner you get homeruns out of your head if you do not have the power, the better for you and your team. More than anything else, people who cannot hit one, ruin more seasons in pursuit of the long ball than anything else. In a later chapter, we will be talking about some ways to maximize what kind of hitter you are.

Chapter 6

: End loaded vs. balanced bats and other hype

I used to hate swinging end loaded bats myself, I mean hey they feel heavier, so why do that to yourself and lose bat speed I thought. Wrong. For one thing, it is getting increasingly difficult to find a true max end-loaded bat. Bat manufacturers know they perform better, so not wanting to have all their bats banned they put out more balanced bats now.

But here are the facts though and much of this has to do with bat speed. We will talk about initial bat speed and after contact bat speed. Initial bat speed is greater using a balanced bat there is no doubt about this. I define initial bat speed as everything before ball contact. However, this is not the speed, which is important for distance hitting. For strictly base hitting balanced is fine and even better than end loaded, because the batter has more control with a balanced bat. I am not saying you cannot hit a homerun with a balanced bat, as you know you can, but for ten or twenty more feet than you are hitting now you want end loaded and the following is why:

After contact bat speed, can actually increase using an end-loaded bat, or at least stay the same or not decrease as much as balanced does. This is because bat weight which is closer to the hands, is easier to control than weight that is out towards the end of the bat. Try to check your swings with a balanced bat, then try it with an end load and you will see it is much harder to stop an end load. It is all about physics.

Now having said all of this and you decide to go end loaded what weight do you choose? You may want to go an ounce or two lighter than you normally use to get the same feel as a balanced bat. If you use a 26oz. bat then you cannot go lighter I realize this, but try and get used to the end load feel and you will love it after a time. Now the problem may come for you to find a true end loaded bat.

Even bats that come from the manufacturers may not really come in what we call "max-end loaded", which is a load that takes up less space at the end of the bat, than a stock load. For example, a stock load and even some factory end loads, may take up an inch or two of bat space, while a denser, more compact max-load can take half that, which will result in a bigger sweet spot to hit with. This alone can make a huge difference in bat performance of 10-20 extra feet in distance. So where do you get one of these?

As time goes by it is becoming more and more difficult to find these bats, as the manufacturers try and keep away from their bats being banned by the governing sanctions, such as ASA, USSSA, NSA etc. For example, the original "Miken Ultra maxload" was not on the market long before it was banned, so Miken came out with the "Ultra 2" which was a balanced version of the original. Supposedly, it was not as hot, but as just about everyone knows it was very hot, so it is also banned just about everywhere now just like the original. Nevertheless, it is indisputable that the original did in fact hit farther because of the end load.

Ray Demarini used to tell people the perfect bat weight for a softball player was 28oz. I tend to agree with this. Even though I am 6'1" 215 lbs., I like to use a light bat. Depending on which model I am swinging I will use anywhere between a 26 and 28. However, bat weights are personal preference, so do not listen to anyone but you. I have found when I am hitting say 100 or so hits off the tee, I use more energy when using a 28oz. bat than a 26oz., so I go lighter to go longer and hit more.

It is amazing what a difference just one or two ounces will make over the long haul. Some people swear a heavier bat will allow one to hit the ball farther because of the greater mass. I do not think it is necessarily the mass, but after contact bat speed, which comes into play when going heavier. So yes heavier may result in more distance, but its only because, that heavier bat is harder to slow down after contact. Of course, a bigger barrel and sweet spot, which may come on certain bats, never hurts. Ok, now what about all this bat hype and this one hits farther than that one etc.

I have to tell you after the dozens and dozens of new bats I tested recently; it was a bit surprising and disappointing at the same time for me to find they all came in around the same distance. Oh sure there are a couple which stood out, but for the most part they all made a good showing for themselves.

I am not going to list all the bats here, because reviews are ever changing and new models are coming out all the time. The bottom line on reviews is they are subjective and everyone likes what they like. Some people are die-hard Demarini, Worth, Miken, etc. etc., people who will not use anything else and who am I or anyone to tell them it is not a good bat?

I have found the most important thing about bats is because the distances are so close on the top five or ten, feel, sweet spot, price and durability should be the determining factor for their bat choice. I have hit all the top bats over the 320 foot fence I practice on, so which do I use? The one which feels the best in my hands, lasts the longest, and has the best value. For me right now, that bat is Anderson for ASA and Combat B1 for non-ASA, and no they have not paid me to say this.

I am sure it bothers you as it has me, to have had your expensive $300+ bats either banned recently or had to be recertified which gives you back a bat which does not perform like the original.

Any of you association heads affiliated with the ASA, USSSA, NSA or pick your governing body which may read this; I have a message for you from the thousands of little guys who help pay your inflated salaries. Stop messing with our bats and balls! Enough is enough.

They could have just CHANGED THE BALLS and they know it. The fact that they let senior players over sixty years old use Miken Ultras, proves that safety was not their concern at all. What sense does it make that the guys with the slowest reflexes get to use the most lethal bats? Yeah they are real concerned with safety.

It looks like there is at least a start of some sense to this bat rating system, which has come late, but finally here in some form. There is a new MPH rating, that the new bats will now have and nothing rated over 98 MPH as of July 04 will be legal to use in the ASA. This is a bit of fresh air, brought to a stinky situation that was a long time coming but still is not perfect.

I have already seen some of these ratings on old bats and they are almost right on, except for the bats that get hotter after they are broken in.

In addition, they let Demarini/Wilson skate on these ratings, which is a travesty as well. They are letting them get away with a 'barely legal rating' on all their bats. It just shows you who is tied in with who and where the money flows. The ultimate weapon single wall 'barely legal'? I do not think so. Of course this is a marketing ploy.

So no rating system is perfect including this one, but still it is better than what we had before. One more thing that the ASA and maybe others are doing as well is performing a ring test. This is where they run a paper or plastic ring over the barrel and of it does not make it over the entire barrel because of even a slight wave they won't let you use the bat.

Just another travesty the ASA and others are saddling the players with. I think this one will sink the ASA eventually, as players are not going to keep standing for these regulations that are draining their patience and pocketbooks at the same time.

Last word on end loaded bats is, if you are playing ASA and using mush balls with core 44

375lbs. compression, then the only way to get more distance is with an end load and or going heavier. There is only one exception I have found so far to this rule and that is the Anderson Rocket tech ck, which has been tuned for these balls like no other.

Chapter 7:

Juiced Bats

Here is a hot potato, but it would not have to be so if what we were just taking about in the previous chapter was not happening. Juiced, enhanced, loaded, altered, customized, doctored bats all mean the same thing. Someone altered the bat, to change it from its original factory settings if you will, to make the bat perform better.

While many of these bats cannot be used in sanctioned leagues, there are many new non- sanctioned leagues starting to sprout up all over because of the banning mess, where they can be used along with your own personal use or in H.R. derbies and the like. Some people call the people who do this bat doctors, I call them my friends and they should be thanked, not vilified.

My case and point is as follows; John Q. Public goes down to the store, buys a $400 PST, and because he is a true competitor buys a $300 Miken and a $300 TPS Genesis. Now before these bats where banned, they had the proper markings ASA and USSSA approved BPF 1.20 etc. John goes along and un-wraps them and uses the bats very much to his liking, when lo and behold someone comes and tells him he cannot use them any longer, because they exceeded some bat, ball speed test these zipper heads in these associations decided to come up with AFTER THE FACT.

Now John cannot go back and get his money back because the bats are used and the best scenario he is given is to send them back to be recertified and in the case of Miken this was never an option. Therefore, John sends the bats back and gets back from the manufacturer two pieces of junk he never paid for to begin with. If he knew ahead of time this was going to happen to his $1000 worth of bats, he would have never paid that amount.

In fact, he would not have bought those bats at all; he would have chosen another, which he was more hopeful would not be banned! Of course, John does not know the future either, but what he now knows is someone just screwed him out of $1000 worth of bats and he is holding garbage in his hands! So Mr. and Mrs. ASA or USSSA in charge, don't be surprised when the people who you just stole $1000 of their hard earned money from, rise up and tell you they don't want to hear from you again, unless you give them their money back, or let them use the original bat, which you had originally said was OK to use.

In addition, do not be surprised when they turn to other remedies like having their bats juiced to perform like the ones you just banned. Finally do not be surprised when the big lawyer comes a knocking and slaps a class action lawsuit on your association.

The next time you decide on allowing your bogus approval stamp on another bat do you think maybe you can test the bat first, not after we have spent the money? We the people sincerely hope so. Ok I got it out of my system I think. Thanks for letting me ramble.

Ok, back to what you can do, to make yourself more competitive. I know some will say this is cheating, but this is only true if using these in sanctioned leagues, which I do not condone doing by the way. You may want to know what juicing a bat is exactly and some of the work, which can be accomplished to make your bat perform better.

Now first realize juicing the bat is going to void the warranty, so do not even think about returning a doctored bat to the manufacturer. They do not want to know anything about this and they have nothing to do with it. Once you get a bat done up, it will be your responsibility to use it as you see fit and in the proper venues.

Some bats you can detect that alterations have been performed, depending on who did the work and what model the bat it is. Some models are near to impossible to juice because of the difficult to replicate or remove end caps. Some are easy to do and completely undetectable to even the trained eye, that the bat has been worked on after the fact.

The end cap is removed and the bat has its weight distribution changed from being more hand weighted to more end weighted, plain and simple. This alone will make the bat perform much better. Then the walls of the bat can be thinned to make the walls flex easier, which will in turn make the bat weaker, but perform better with harder balls. On mush balls thinning the walls does not help at all and can even hurt.

In some bats, rods are inserted into the handles, which either can be removed or shortened which will change the weight composition to more of an end load. This alone helps enhance the performance and weight distribution, which is the crux of juicing a bat.

There are few other things, which can be done, but these are the main ones, which will get you the performance you seek. A lot of this also depends on the balls you are hitting with, but for me right now in ASA, the Anderson Rocket Tech CK is tops, with the freak coming in a close 2nd and the 375 3rd. Also I do not recommend juicing a RT CK because of the way the walls are tuned and it is already end loaded perfectly.

There is one more thing you can do to help with the performance of your high tech bat and that is to purchase a bat warmer. More than just a gimmick, these will keep the surface of the bat barrel well above the recommended sixty degree temperature that all bat manufacturers say not to use their bats under.

I just picked up a new bat warmer line that is so good it actually keeps the barrel hot, not just warm for four to six hours. Believe me; it makes a huge difference in greater distance and durability on these expensive bats, whether they are composite or aluminum. The fact is any material becomes less flexible and more brittle in cooler weather. I use mine even in 70-80 degree weather and it makes a big difference in the flexibility of the walls.

Chapter 8:

Ball Information- Ball hype

I will try here to simplify a complex issue. We all know about the hype surrounding bats, but let us look at the balls now. It is probably more confusion rather than hype, but it should not be so. COR or (Coefficient of Reflection), is the rate at which a ball will reflect back after being cast against an immovable object. So the higher the COR number, the higher the reflectivity or the higher the bounce if you will. Core 47 has a higher bounce than a core 40. However, COR is not as important as ball compression, although if you could choose a core 47 with low compression, this would be a good ball for a stiff walled bat (i.e. Techzilla ck or the RTCK) which was frequency tuned for them.

Unfortunately, low compression balls are normally paired up with 40 COR. This is why it is important to separate the two. The compression is much more important and it breaks down like this: 375lb. comp balls are softer or "compress" more than 525 lb. balls. It takes 525lbs. of pressure per square inch to compress a 525lb. Ball a 1/4". It takes only 375lbs. of pressure to compress a 375lb. ball 1/4". So the higher the compression, the harder the ball and the harder the ball the farther it will fly WITH THE RIGHT BAT. What is the right bat? Well let us look at a bit more.

If you could choose the ultimate ball for lets say a Miken ultra, which is an extreme flex bat, it would be a high compression 525lb. ball with 40 COR as opposed to 47 COR. Most times though 525's are paired up with 47 COR, but it is not that COR that hit the ball so far, it is the hardness or compression.

Now on a stiffer walled bat like the Techzilla CK, the best ball match would be 47 COR and low375lb. compression. Again, you do not see this ball too often because usually low COR is matched with low compression, but that would be a more ideal match for a stiff walled bat.

I am not saying the ultra does not still hit mush balls well either, but it is indisputable that it hits the harder balls much, much farther. I also am not saying a TZCK will hit a mush ball as far as an ultra would hit a harder ball, but the physics are what I am trying to point out here.

Now let's look at a low compression ball 375lbs. and a bat with a lot of flex i.e.: ultra, rocket tech, synergy, PST, etc. Typically, a low compression ball and a bat with a lot of flex is not a good combination especially over time, because over time the ball gets even more flexible. The leagues and sanctioning bodies know this and is why they are going to these balls.

A better pairing is those above named bats and a high compression 525lb. ball. Hard ball meets'soft high flex' bat = long hit. A better bat for the low compression 375lb. balls is something that does not flex as much and this is how the world record of 530 some feet was broken back in the 70's. A 'hard' bat (no flex), was used with a ball more like what the low compression balls are becoming. Back in the 1970s, the balls flexed incredibly and made of a type of "Surilyn". The flex on the ball was incredible and rivaled what a super ball is like today. They quickly were outlawed and now the bats of today are the focus of the banning as the balls were in the 70's.

So now, we as players should find out what compression balls are being used in our leagues and tournaments so we can match a better bat to the ball we are using. In fact, a better bat now for the low comp balls, which are becoming more prevalent, may in fact be the bats of long ago which did not flex as much. What new bats out there now do not flex as much? The Techzilla ck comes to mind immediately.

It flex's for the very hard hitter, but for the average hitter who cannot flex it as much, it may be exactly the bat that the Dr. ordered for these low compression balls, along with the RTCK which was made to hit them as well. Now I am not saying this combination will hit a ball as far as an Ultra hit a high compression ball. Nothing will. The truth is we may never see this kind of performance again, who knows?

Now having said all of this what is the real difference in distance between a low compression and a high compression ball. My experience has been only around 10-30 ft. It may not sound like a lot, but for some it is the difference between hitting a HR and hitting a long fly out. In addition, different ball manufacturers will make a difference in performance. There are too many to mention here, but suffice it to say, some companies put out pure junk while others even though they are low compression still are hard enough. I have found a new company called pro nine that makes a great low compression ball that flies farther because of the semi-raised stitching, plus they stay harder longer in comparison to others.

Lastly, you need to realize this low compression ball mess is just that. Really, not many bats perform all that well with them, except the bats I have mentioned, so this is a very short list right now. This is why the leagues are moving in this direction. The truth is there may never be a bat again which will hit a low compression ball as far as the ultra hit a high compression ball.

For example if you could hit a high comp ball with an ultra say 350ft.(like many people can), then chances are you could hit a low comp ball with the ultra 325 ft. Does this mean the Ck's will hit the low comp. ball 350 ft.? It depends on your bat speed. You may get 325 ft., but still they are a better match and they are legal to use. All of the high flex bats on the market hit the low comps the same, which is not very good. Again, I am talking about distance here and not base hits.

This is another reason end loads are becoming so important, because regardless of the ball being used, the end load will get you more distance. There are currently only two ASA bats listed in the top ten, in the bat reviews categories for pop and distance; all others are non ASA bats. One is the RTCK in the top ten for pop and the other is the original Freak (not the 98) for distance. This makes the RTCK even more amazing considering they rate it at only 98 MPH. The reason for this is, composites in the ASA have to be detuned and hand weighted to pass the test, while the aluminum RTCK was actually juiced from the factory, so which one would you rather swing?

Chapter 9:

Baseball and Fast pitch Timing

I am grouping these together, because in some instances the ball travel speeds in these sports are identical. This may or may not be important, but it is still nice to know what you are facing. If slow-pitch softball is a hitter's game and it is or should be, then baseball is surely a pitchers game along with fast pitch softball. Runs are a bit more at a premium than they are in slow-pitch this is certain. Therefore, homeruns and extra base hits can and do play a much bigger part of the game, where runs are more scarce.

In baseball, the pitch can be coming at different angles depending on the pitchers release point. In fast pitch, it is constant because the release is always from the underhand position, but one exception to the angle, is the rise pitch. While most are coming in level, the rise starts low and comes in high. This will not affect your timing but simply your pitch selection skills.

Before we get into timing these pitches, I just want to cover a few changes you may want to make in the batter's box etc. for baseball or fast pitch and a few other things you may want to consider. In slow-pitch you can really stand anywhere in the box and be successful, but in baseball and fast pitch because the ball is coming in so quickly, you may want to consider standing towards the front of the batter's box to guard against balls in the dirt and in front of you. The only advantage to being deep in the box would be to have more time to judge a pitch and see it longer, but I don't think this outweighs the advantages of being towards the front, because I don't think two or three feet will make much difference. Also like in slow-pitch, you should have more opportunities to swing at more pitches for strikes, than being back.

Being an aggressive hitter and bat speed comes into play even more in both fast pitch and baseball. You simply do not have as much reaction time to play with because of the higher speeds. You will be swinging late the majority of the time, not early. If you keep your hands back and check your swing on balls, you will rarely if ever, be swinging too early. Remember: Start the body early, the hands will follow at the proper time and simply check or stop your swing on balls.

OK let us start with your timing trigger for baseball. You want to start your motion to swing (your legs) right before the pitcher actually releases the ball. The best way is to focus on the spot that the ball will come from, BEFORE RELEASE. Some people call this a slot. This will be when the pitching hand is ALL THE WAY BACK fully extended before coming forward to release.

In fast pitch, this is right before the final down motion of the windmill action. No matter what a pitcher is doing before this does not matter. Do not be concerned with all the different idiosyncrasies a pitcher may have because they all have to come to a traditional release point.

There is no return for the pitcher at this point so it is safe for you to start your body and weight transfer by lifting your front foot at this point. How high you will lift or stride forward is personal preference, but the general rule is the bigger the stride and step the more time it will take to complete, so this must be compensated for, by an earlier trigger. Then while still keeping the hands back drive back towards the ball at pitch release or no later than a foot or so out of the hand. When your front foot touches down to complete your stride, your hands will now come through the hitting zone for ball contact out in front of you, with your entire body, both shoulders included, behind the bat and imaginary lead arm line.

Just to reiterate, in fast pitch softball the timing trigger to start the motion to swing, should be on the downward motion of the last windmill action when the ball can be seen in the hand, behind the pitcher with the arm fully extended. There is no return or stopping the pitcher from releasing the ball at this point. Between this point and the balls release right near the side of the body is a distance of two feet or so. This is the time to start the legs. Again not bringing the hands through the zone yet, but getting better prepared with maximum force, for when you actually do.

Ok now in slow-pitch I told you want to count off two seconds in your head to ball contact. In baseball and fast pitch, this is going to have to be shortened up a bit obviously. Therefore, what you do is watch the pitchers motion and release on the fastballs and the changeups etc. during other players at bats and pre game warm ups etc. and simply come up with a word in your head, which will equal that span of time to bat contact.

On a fastball for example, you might just want to say something quick like "swing" or "aswing" or make something else up which takes longer to say on a changeup like "hit you now." You can use your imagination I am sure. You can either start these words at ball release or before. If you start before then it will have to be a longer word or words naturally. You may want to first perfect the timing on a fastball then try a changeup or off-speed pitch will be slightly different. On a knuckle ball, you might say "what the H- E- double hockey stick is that" and so on. That was my one big joke for the entire book; I hope you found it funny.

Remember no matter what you choose to do in fast-pitch or baseball; it must be much quicker than what I spoke about in slow-pitch, so bat speed and compactness of the entire motion to swing can be much more important depending on the type of hitter you choose to be. Many of the professionals still choose the more time consuming motion with the big leg kick etc. Because this takes more time, they are starting those motions much earlier in the pitchers delivery. If you do not believe me just watch them on TV. Some of them in fact are in almost a state of constant motion, but those ever-important hands are back all the while. This is why you should perfect as well.

When the young players are just starting out it will be more like slow-pitch, because the kids are not yet throwing at the high speeds as they will later on in their development. The weight transfer at the younger ages can be much more difficult to teach because their understanding just is not there yet, but for those who can it is important.

How many kids have you seen swing with arms only? For those who just do not get it, try to get them to at least take some form of step or stride forward to the ball. If this must be accomplished by having them temporarily practice the feet together stance then do so, unless you as a coach or parent are content in having them hit weakly to the pitcher or infielders. As the pitch-speed increases and they get older and better and they have learned the weight transfer, then they can widen the stance for more balance and power.

My daughter started playing softball at age nine and she is now ten. Since day one, she decided she was going to swing like Dad without me even saying a word to her, so she took this big old step just like me and she has been crushing the ball to everyone's amazement. Everything she hits is hard.

She has only played in ten games and ten practices so far and is already hitting like a champion. She led the league in hitting and the team went on to win their second Championship two years in a row. At this age winning is not what is important, but this can be a tough thing for a child to fathom after they win a championship.

Chapter 10:

Advanced hitting techniques

What we have talked about so far, is good enough for you to become a truly elite hitter. I just wanted you to know there are other techniques out there and they all can work to one extent or another to your benefit. You can add to and fit many different styles of hitting into my technique and system. These next few following techniques would be more for slow-pitch softball players who have more time to react to a pitch. You may have seen some of these in action by a few players.

The first one is what I call my 'Mother Load' technique. Actually, you may not have seen this one and it is the easiest advanced technique to do. What it allows for and does is even more weight transfer. It guarantees a more powerful weight transfer, so if you decide you need more power and distance this may be for you.

You will want to try this in practice off the tee first. However, it is as simple as this; everything else we discussed about the two-second count etc. will still apply to this naturally because that never changes. Remember on the launch when we said you would be lifting your front foot up and back to start the weight transfer. With this technique, you will first be moving your BACK foot at pitch release (the one closest to the catcher) and usually planted, back straight towards the catcher six to twelve inches or whatever is comfortable. THEN you will resume everything else the same as before with the front foot launching up and back as usual.

You may want to count, as your back foot is coming back one-Mississippi, then when you drive back towards the ball the other way, count two-Mississippi to ball contact. This fits perfectly in with what I teach and it provides maximum momentum and weight transfer. I just found this hitting off the tee one day and I noticed that every time I did it, I hit the ball with a lot more force.

The only thing with this technique is you will have to be concerned with your batter's box positioning a bit more. If you are standing deep in the box, you may need to consider moving up to the middle or front for this. In addition, this takes more time to do so it will be imperative you start at pitch release otherwise, you will be contacting the ball too late. Another thing about this technique that is great is even though you are moving your lower body quite a bit; you can still keep your head and upper body quiet and on the ball, as they say.

The next one I have no idea if it has a name or who came up with it, but it is fun to watch players, who have mastered this. For the most part they are very good hitters and have incredible focus because they are walking, scooting, or what have you in the batter's box while the pitch is in the air.

Some take two steps some take more, but what they are doing is allowing themselves to be able to hit just about any pitch in the zone or even shallow. They must start back deep in the box however to do this correctly. The best way again to practice this is of course off the batting tee. If you want to try this or a variation, do not forget the two second head count.

There may be other non-conventional ways of hitting a slow-pitch softball, which you may find on your own. As long as they net you the desired result, why not try them. Someone can tell you this or that may not be sound mechanics, but I would simply ask them, what are you hitting again? .500? Oh, ok Thanks. It is really somewhat comical when people for one reason or another would read or hear something and say that cannot work without ever having tried it.

Speaking of averages in slow-pitch this is a good place for me to address this. I am sure you may be wondering what in fact is considered an average that is good etc. In my experience with slow- pitch, people who are just starting out hit anywhere between .400 and .500. In addition, from playing on many teams of different levels over the years I have found .500 seems to be the number, which would denote being an average hitter.

Above .600, now you are getting into the area of the hitters who know what they are doing and have more confidence. .700 and above is what many consider to be an 'A' type of hitter and I would agree with this. The team average on many of the championship teams I have had the pleasure to coach and play on was .550, but we had exceptional defense. Really, our defense was as good as you can get and our bats were just slightly above average. Though overall we would not have been considered to be an A team, we had beaten some over the years. I am sure we were classified as more of a B or C team. Many of these classifications can also depend on the location of the country you play in too.

Chapter 11:

Great Drills and Training

Here are some ideas, which you may have never thought of or tried before. I know there are many ways you can train and there as many drills etc. as there are ideas. When it comes to team practice, it can tend to become a little boring if you do not spice it up every now and again. I will also discuss some individual drills you can do for yourself to help your hitting.

Rather than just the standard one person hits until they get tired and everyone else stands around watching, try and maximize practice time by having some sort of limit on the cuts the batter may be allowed to take the first round, so everyone gets a chance etc. Also in practice nowadays the pitcher can be very vulnerable in these days of hi-tech equipment, so they really should almost be wearing full catchers gear or hockey equipment or something to protect them.

The difference in the number of hits in practice compared to a game is substantial, so therefore there is a greater chance the pitcher will be hit in practice. Why not give your regular game pitcher a break and have everyone take a chance and throw some. Even better yet is team use of the batting tee, but if your team is anything like mine, you will have those who will not want to use it. However, this is the single most efficient use of batting and practice time you could ever find. Imagine all the players only swinging at strikes. A batting machine would be nice too, but those are expensive, do not always throw strikes and they are not as portable as one would like. Some of the best teams I have ever faced come to find out said they use the batting tee in TEAM PRACTICE.

Now for some game situation drills etc. Let us say you have 15 people show up to a practice (dream on) or at least at the beginning of the season you may. Instead of having fourteen people on the field at once, why not bat five as a group as if they were a team and let them hit until they make three outs.

Then you switch it up on hit another five players etc. If you have 13, use three and so forth. This is a great game situation drill and similar to a scrimmage. Another variation of this would be one batter, but they only get three outs then go on to the next. The reason why I like this one so much is it gets people thinking about the base hit more than the homerun. In addition, just to survive and stretch their batting time out they will try to get a hit.

If you only have let us say eight people show up for practice (this is more common), then you will have to get more creative, like hitting to one field is an out and so on. If it is one thing an outfielder cannot stand its people hitting to the open field where they are not, because they are expected to run over and shag all of those balls.

Pepper is one you probably know about, but if you don't, it is simply having any number of players line up and they throw pitches into a batter who usually check swings or half swings the ball back to the people in line. You can do this quickly to speed it up. The distance from the line to the batter should not be very far. Probably thirty feet or so should do.

Here are some great drills for individual use. These will help develop your swing using muscle memory and become a more aggressive hitter, which is the crux of the GHS.

Muscle memory is a phrase you may hear a lot about. It is defined as physically going through a certain motion so much it becomes a part of you never to be forgotten or undone, much like riding a bike.

The first drill I like to do is simple, as most drills are. You are going to go through your motion to swing pretending the ball has been released from the pitchers hand. However, for the first one, do not complete the follow-thru. I want you to check your swing right in the middle of hitting zone. Why practice this? Because this is something, you need to be doing more of in the game. This will help stop you from swinging at balls, like nothing else you have ever tried.

If you do not practice it, you will not do it in the game. In addition, it is a great drill for the Perfect Timing Technique (PTT). You want to go through this motion as many times as you can in a five-minute period. You can do this in front of the tee and check the swing right before ball contact or away from the tee if you do not have one. In addition, you want to go through the two- second head count from launch all the while you are doing this.

One of the coolest things about this drill and the PTT itself is you can go through spring training never have seen a live pitch and get into the game ready for anything with perfect timing. This may be a hard thing to fathom, but it works like magic. Never underestimate the power of the 'dry' swing in practice. It is crucial for muscle memory in the batters box and off to the side before the game.

You should always be taking the opportunity to go through your swing whenever you can and for as many times as you can. Too many people stand around talking before the game when they should be swinging. People rush to get five swings in before the game from the pitcher when they could be taking dozens of dry cuts, which are even more profitable.

Ok More drills. This one is excellent as well. Go through your motion to swing again, except keep your hands back all the way (just as always) even when your front foot touches down. So with this one, you will not even be coming to the check swing position. Here you are going through your weight transfer only. What you will find is breaking your swing down into segments helps isolate each important part of it to solidify it in your subconscious. In the next chapter, you will see just how important the subconscious really is.

Some great training exercises I have found to be most beneficial to me are as follows. My favorite is Rollerblading or ice-skating. These two will work the same muscles in the legs and I am sure most of you will opt for the rollerblading, but which ever you choose, give yourself a good fast workout which makes the muscles burn.

If you have a place to rollerblade, with a slight incline go for it and yes I do mean uphill. If you only have level ground to skate on then consider wearing a weighted backpack or ankle weights to make those muscles work. You only need twenty to thirty minutes of this kind of training for it to be effective and three to four times a week will do fine.

The key to this exercise is the burn. With this kind of intensity, you will fly around those base pads. What you do not want is the kind of workout that is long and drawn-out. You may burn calories, but that is not the goal unless you need to lose weight too. If you need to do this then you should do both, have some long workouts and short. On the longer workouts, you are not really looking for the muscle burn feeling, but instead more of endurance type of workout.

Another great way to burn and build those legs is a bike ride, but again not long enduring rides, but the short intense kind up hills and such. Put it in low gear and burn it up!

If you are a runner fine, but make those runs short and fast with lots of sprints. The Stairmaster or mountain climber is better for hitting than the treadmill is, so there are many options for you. This is not meant to be an all-inclusive list, I am sure there are many other things you can think of to do for yourself.

Ok, this is for the lower body which is by the way the most important to develop for hitting. On the upper body, you do not need to have superman arms to hit a ball. Weight lifting is great too and I used to do a lot of it myself, but it is not as important as flexibility is. If you can have both great, but you do not need to be pumped up like Mr. Universe.

For the forearms however, wrist curls are great as well as the grips for developing forearms too. Strong forearms will give the bat a much lighter feel and increase bat control substantially. Sounds like I might be describing Popeye, but I will bet he was a heck of a ball player.

Chapter 12:

Are you Mental?

Well we all are to one extent or another. The subconscious mind controls the physical body. This is why muscle memory is so important. However, not just any muscle memory, the correct kind. What I mean here is this. Think about team batting practice for a moment. At the average team practice, you have some poor soul who has to endure throwing hundreds of pitches, in sometimes-oppressive heat, to ten players or so and they are expected to throw all strikes.

This of course does not happen and if you are lucky, you may see 50% strikes. What does the batter do with the balls? They try to hit them, for the most part, because they do not want to waste the rest of the teams' time. The players in the field may actually be yelling at the batter to swing if he is not or at the pitcher if more strikes are not being thrown to their liking.

The pitchers in many cases are just trying to protect themselves and thereby will subconsciously be throwing balls all over the place. I know I have done it too many times to count. Very rarely do you see a pitch right down the middle where you want. Does anyone see a problem with this scenario? I do and it is huge. I know there may be a few of you very disciplined hitters who hold off on the balls and never swing at even one in practice, but you are a small minority.

Therefore, the problem for most of us is we get into bad habits and the wrong muscle memory of swinging at balls in practice, which results in ugly swings of all sorts. Should anyone be surprised if we do not bring bad habits into the next game? This may be why there are more .500 hitters than there are .600 & .700. In fact, I am convinced of it. If you are not yet, do not worry I will be convinced for you.

Here is another reason why muscle memory is so important. You will not always be focused100% of the time, so in these cases of non-focus you want something else to take over for your shortcoming. Muscle memory will do it for you, WHEN you start at the correct time and we all now know when this is now.

This is how the day both teams were blinded by the sun and I was the only one smoking line drives everywhere. My subconscious and muscle memory took over for the lack of focus and eye contact, which was lacking because of the sun in my eyes.

The subconscious is such a powerful tool that you need to harness to become truly great. You are what you think you are and you are what you eat etc. There is much truth in these statements.

If you want to get more base hits then you are going think about them more. Visualizing a base hit is the mental key to hitting one. However, the need to be specific here is paramount. Too often, we generalize these things to our detriment. Here is a great example: You have a pitch that is coming towards the inside of the plate, you have already started your motion to swing and now there is only one more thing to do. You need to think about where you are going to hit it. You want to maximize the location of this pitch by sending it back to the location from which it came. Do not waste an inside pitch and try to hit it to the opposite field. Some people do, but it is not going to be hit as hard as if you pull the ball.

Other side is, do not try to pull an outside pitch. Now you may want to be even more specific than what field you are going to hit it. How about this, will you hit it through the infield holes such as down the line, in-between third base and short? Of course, the middle is a huge hole and then on the first base side you have the opposite of the third base, with corresponding holes and the line.

Pitch height should dictate whether you would shoot it through a hole, or go for the top spin line drive over the infielder's heads or lastly go for the long ball. The low pitch should be hit through the holes; the medium height should go for more airtime, think line drive. The high pitch can be sent for the long ride home.

It is difficult to hit a low pitch for homerun distance without dropping the back shoulder or lunging at the ball and losing out on the level swing. This is because the bottom half of the ball must be struck for backspin and this is made more difficult on a low pitch.

Again, thinking about where exactly you should hit a pitch is the key to actually doing it. Many people say I only want to hit the ball hard and this is NOT good enough.

I know plenty of people who hit the ball hard right at someone time after time and they wonder how this is happening. This is simply because they did not specify in their heads beforehand where they were going to hit it. This proves how powerful the mind is.

This also is the difference between how the pros think and focus and how the rest of us do. Many professional athletes go through special training just on the art of concentration and focus. Whole days and seminars on the subject are attended in many places.

Roger Clemens has focus down to a science and this no doubt has led too much of his success. He says he can block out 50,000 screaming fans, the umpire and the catcher and only focus on the catcher's mitt.

I am sure he may have even taken this a step further like Ted Williams did in hitting, to focus on the center of the catcher's mitt. There is little doubt that Roger has become what he has from being not only a power type pitcher, but also a control type of pitcher as well.

Therefore, we can see here how the mental aspect of the game is even more important than the physical. It also extends into other parts of your game in a big way. Let us look at for a moment the other side of the game. Base running for example. Does anyone know of times which you or someone else wasn't thinking right, or maybe not thinking at all when it comes to running the bases? Base coaches, which we will discuss more about later, cannot be held responsible if you decide to run full bore and always try to take the extra base when you should not.

Chapter 13:

Pitching Tips

This is a subject near and dear to my heart because I pitched for two years a while back now, but I loved it while I did it, especially the first year. I threw a very high arc always around twelve feet and just had a blast doing so. My second year my talent somehow went south which had something to do with my fear of being hit, but the first year was something to behold.

I will be also addressing fast pitch pitching very quickly and I will leave baseball to someone else more adept than I, but these tips will help just about any kind of pitcher, because many defensive strategies can be applied across the board.

I always wanted to be a pitcher. In many respects, the pitcher is like the general of the team. You shortstops can just chill here. The pitcher controls whether or not the balls are going to be hit to the left side the right or up the middle. Most good pitchers try to keep the latter happening as little as possible. Just the simplest of strategies can quickly propel you to top billing in your league or area. The pitchers who master the following are the best of the best.

I am not talking how you need to master your curveball, knuckle, screwball, change-up or what have you, not that this is not important, but it is separate from the following. It is the other things about your game which you will need to master first, before you can move on to the more complex.

For example, let us say you have the best arm in the state. You throw a 100 MPH fastball, a nasty knuckle ball and a great change-up. The problem is you have no control, throw all your pitch's right down the middle of the plate with no game strategy to help the other infielders etc.

You will not last long as a pitcher throwing like this. First let us look at where you want to throw the ball for different kinds of batters, how to work a count, then we will talk about defensive positioning and some other issues.

When I pitched slow-pitch, I thought it was easy. I threw the maximum arc allowed; I threw the ball to hit the corners and worked the balls deep and shallow. I always tried to keep the batters off stride whenever I could, because good hitters will hit in slow-pitch no matter what you do.

Therefore, you are trying to get the average batter to hit it where you want, not where they want. The batter that is more concerned with you and what your idiosyncrasies may be is the one that is easier to control.

I added a nice twist to my pitching which was after I released the ball I would back peddle as fast as I could to close up the middle. This worked like a charm, because it was like adding a fifth infielder. Two seconds after pitch release, I was back in front of the second base bag. This was murder on the calves but it worked so good we held opposing teams to three runs and less on a regular basis. We already had a great infield already this just made it invincible.

I think another reason it worked so good was it took the batter out of his element and broke their focus. In many respects it just plain old freaked them out, because there was not too many pitchers doing it. In fact, I had not known anyone in the area who was doing it and I just thought it was a cool idea not even knowing how effective it would actually be.

Another great thing about this technique is it is safer for the pitcher to be farther away from the ball. At the time, I had not even thought or cared about this part of it. Bottom line is more pitchers should be doing it, just make sure calve raises become part of your training regimen. This of course is for the slow pitch pitcher who has lots of time to come back into position.

Ok, back to some simple stuff. Follow-thru is a very important in pitching just like hitting. The underhand pitch is more likened to a bowling movement than anything else is and in bowling follow thru is where it is at for accuracy. The quick pitch we will get to in a minute, but your bread and butter pitch for location should be a pitch where you will continue after the balls release from the hand and straight on up just as they do in bowling. This will give you the high arc and better location then just snapping the ball quickly with no follow through. Actually, the high arc pitch is a good one to start with to get the first pitch strike. After that, you can mix it up with a quick pitch or backspin or side release.

It is imperative you try to keep your shoulders and upper body straight up during this process. Dropping the shoulder is just as bad in pitching as it is in hitting. Dropping or releasing from an uneven keel will result in no control, so whenever you go off, take a big deep breath, start again slow and follow-thru with the arm. The arm must stay as close to the body as you can to use your body as a guide to throw straight. Try to stand up straight while pitching.

A crouching or bent over is not needed or wanted in softball. If you decide, you are not going to try back stepping after pitch release; you should at least try it on pitches down the middle of the plate. You know the ones where you say to yourself uh oh why did I let that go, after you have released it.

You can also do a variation of this by not back peddling, but taking one or two steps back, to get ready for a shot back up the middle.

Pitching strategy is fun and here are some tips to pitch to different kinds of hitters. Let us say you are facing a power team or a power hitter. I remember a game we were being destroyed to the tune of 17-0 and we had a pitcher who was just grooving the balls over the plate. I finally said to him start throwing them short, he did and they kept swinging but now they were hitting weakly all over the place.

We came back and won the game, it was one of those classics. So pitching short or shallow will negate power. Of course, if they are disciplined hitters you may not get them to bite, but many will.

If the batter is standing deep in the box this is another signal to pitch short. Batters in the front of the box, throw deep. Batters standing very close to the plate, throw inside. Batters, far from the plate throw outside. These are general rules, which work great.

If you throw a first pitch strike and he does not bite, the second pitch should be a ball. I would rather throw a first pitch ball myself to get the people who swing at the first pitch as I do. If they do not bite then you will want to come back with a strike. However, whatever you do, do not become predictable. You do not have a fastball to throw so throw everything else you can.

If you have a person who just hit the ball 400ft. last time up, for Pete's sake don't throw him another meat ball. If you have to, walk him, not intentionally, but in some cases you may even want to do that too. I know many whiners who would say, c'mon man let the person hit. Why? Because he is your Goliath we have to let him hit? It is called strategy. If I allow him to hit a bomb every time up, I am the fool not you.

We have a person who is built like Sammy Sosa on our team and he hits like him too, so he does not even need the juiced bats. Anyway, Kyle is walked more than any other player I have ever seen and with good reason. Not only does Kyle hit 350 ft. laser beams he also hits up the middle and everywhere else and has hurt many a player, never intentionally of course. He does it with any bat to boot. If you saw Kyle hit you would walk him too.

One more thing about pitching is there is no steadfast rule, which says the pitcher has to pitch from atop the rubber. Many times the rubber is sticking up higher than you would like and standing on top of it can result it being unbalanced, so in this case at least you would want to stand behind it and just have your front toe touching the rubber. This is a small but important detail.

The pitcher also has other responsibilities such as backing up throws from the outfield and covering first base if the first baseman is far from the bag and will not make it in time for the out. So always, be ready to cover first in these instances.

Is it important to learn about how to throw different kinds of pitches? Backspins, palm balls, knuckles and others. If you can do it then yes, it is a great idea and there are other places to get more on this. Some are easier than others are to learn, but the idea is to try to throw off the batter anyway you can. I never threw anything fancy except the occasional backspin and some different release points, such as down low from the side. You can become an A level pitcher without the fancy stuff in slow-pitch, but every little thing helps, so why not learn as much as you can.

Equipment for a pitcher is not a bad idea nowadays. Some sort of hockey mask or catcher's mask, chest protection, shin guards and cup. Do not be too proud to use this stuff. If I was still pitching and who knows maybe I will again I would definitely use it. Also for practice a pitching screen may be a good team investment for the pitcher to throw from behind.

Chapter 14:

Defensive Tips

The other side of the game, which is super important, is defense. It is every bit as important as offense and the teams, which are good defensively, have a lot less work to do than those who lack in this department. I have played on both kinds of teams.

One had exceptional defense and the other was lacking. The team with exceptional defense averaged only 12 runs a game but we shut down teams with such regularity it was always enough to win. We won the championship four out of five years and eight out of ten and had an undefeated season of 26-0 thrown in there, which is not easy to do in any league.

The team with poor defense averaged 18 runs a game but we gave away as many and lost many games to stupidity and lack of practicing the basics.

I will give you some defensive tips here, which helped me play the various positions I did over the years with much success. I was fortunate enough to be able to play all the positions in my career and liked them all very much. This information may apply more to slow-pitch, but much of it is the same just like in hitting.

I started in the outfield when I was younger and nimbler. However, if one lacks speed in the outfield, they can make up for it in good judgment and smart decisions. I have played with many who always wanted to be the hero and throw the runners out at third base and at home.

The percentage of these plays, which actually end up being completed, is so small that it is never worth the throw to begin with, unless the game is on the line. In slow-pitch, the game is never on the line until the last inning.

When I played the outfield, I tried to play it like an infielder. Watching to where the pitch is being located to the batters is important on getting an early jump on the ball. An inside pitch is normally going to be pulled and so forth. Also knowing your batters is necessary in how you will be positioning yourself.

If you have a lot of speed, you can play a bit shallower in the field then a player who does not have the speed. Stronger arms should be playing down the lines and the speedier fielders should be in the middle positions.

A great trick I used to like to do is play a particular batter a certain way and then when the pitch is in the air move my position closer to where I actually thought the ball was going to go. As previously covered, we know we have two seconds of time to play with so why not use it in a defensive strategy as well as offensive.

Ok let us say you have fielded the ball, so now where are you going to throw it? Do you always have to throw it to the base you think the runner is advancing? No, you do not, nor should you always try.

This next rule is for 90% of all throws from the outfield and to where they should be thrown. I say the super majority of the throws should go into second base and or the cut-off, with just a few exceptions.

There is only one thing I do not like about throwing to the cut off, but it can be overcome with good communication. If the runner has a lot of speed, they can still make it to second if the cutoff person actually cuts the ball off.

However, in general, it is not a bad idea, but the outfielder should still be aggressive and try to throw it to second and let the cutoff and his counterparts make the decision to cut or to throw thru. There needs to be good communication between the cutoff person and the other infielder who is covering second base to let the cutoff know whether to cut or let the ball go.

Therefore, when I hear people say the ball should be thrown at the cutoff, this is not quite correct. The target is to be second base and the cut-off is simply lining up the throw with the possibility of letting the throw go through or be cut off, depending on the situation.

The cut off is to the middle infielders either second baseman or Shortstop. They need to go out into the field to line up the throw to second base. On a hit which goes up the middle and is not very deep, a cut off is not really needed as much as on a deep hit, where it is required almost certainly.

There are many reasons why this is 99% of the time the perfect place to throw to on a base hit. One is to try to keep the force play intact. This cannot be accomplished if the outfielder decides to try to throw out a runner going to third or even worse home plate. The runner going to first will almost certainly try to move up to second and there goes the force play out the window.

You see there are two parts to throwing a runner out. You may have a golden glove in the outfield with the best arm as well, but on the other end of the play; you have another player who has to catch the ball and make the perfect tag. The odds are not in your favor.

The one time you can throw to other bases in trying to throw someone out is on the tag up play unless the bases are full of runners, but even then, you may want to consider it. You have nothing to lose by trying it and with a little luck; the infielders will be backing the play up for you in case of an overthrow.

Here are some basic rules for an outfielder, which can help. Try to throw to the closest base you can, which is usually second base, depending on where you are in relation to it. Another good reason for throwing to second is there are more backups for a possible errant throw.

Outfielders should back one another up at all times, so each can play more aggressively. Communication stating this is important from one outfielder to another. Playing more aggressively in the outfield is as important as being an aggressive hitter. Trying to go after the shallow hit or line drive in the air is smart if you have the proper back up.

OK lets move to the infield. I will start at first, which is where I play now. Being close enough to the bag is important for a couple reasons. You want to be close enough to be able to run to the base for throws of course, but also to guard against hits down the line.

This does depend of course on knowing the team and players you are going up against and knowing what fields they hit. If the team does not hit to your side you can play much closer to the bag than a team, which hits a lot to right field.

When you run to the bag there is no need to have the foot that will stay planted near the base to be on the base. Some play with safety bases now, which is fine, but even with those, it is better to have the side of your foot up against the base then having it on top of the base. You will be able to lunge and stretch farther to the ball and is inherently safer and more comfortable.

Which foot you place up against the base is personal preference, but which ever foot allows you the most stretch is the one you should use, so try them both out to see which is better.

When to start the lunge and or stretch towards the ball is important. You can start this too soon or too late and be all off in the timing not to mention once you commit there is no going back. You need to wait long enough to judge whether the throw is going to need a lunge at all. If it is going short into the dirt, then lunge and stretch for the ball. If it is a high or wide throw, do not lunge at all, because you will have to come off the base to prevent the overthrow.

The first baseman should be ready for the overthrows from the left or left center fielders especially and back up home plate when necessary.

Do you really need a first basemen's mitt? This is personal preference, of course. However, if you are buying it for reasons of more padding then you may want to think twice. In baseball, it is necessary, but in softball, you do not have to use one. I used a 14" outfielder's glove for years with padding which I loved and found very effective especially on ground balls. I have recently switched to a 12.75" baseball outfielders glove by Akadema and I never thought I could play with a smaller glove. Now I love the thing so much it is my new size and the best all around glove I have ever used.

We discussed the pitcher in pitching tips, so no need to rehash here, just make sure you back up the first baseman on hits in the hole or down the line deep. The first baseman may not be able to recover in time to get to the bag. Also back up home and third when needed.

Second base is much like first as far as the distance from the bag you will want to play. The same rules will apply needing to make sure you can get to the bag in time. Hits to the right side of the field will be your queue to go out and line up the throw to second base.

The short stop is the opposite of the second baseman and the play is similar, so I will not go any further with this other than to say, communication is necessary. The shortstop in many cases is the infield general or even field general calling the throws from the outfielders etc. This can be relegated to the second baseman if the shortstop is not vocal enough.

Third base is much like first, except the third baseman can be a little further from the bag in most situations depending on the hitter is and who is on base.

Catching is one of the most overlooked but very important positions, especially in slow-pitch. Many times the person who cannot run and is not quite as good defensively as the other fielders are get stuck with catching, or so this is how they look at it. However, a good catcher can make so much difference in the way things go down.

One thing some of you people who have not played the position, need to be ready for, is the game sometimes comes down right on your shoulders. When the game is on the line and the throw comes home, you want to be ready to make the catch and tag.

Also a good catcher should know the batters just as well or maybe even better than the pitcher, or at the very least have some sort of signal set up before hand to let the pitcher know how deep or shallow the player is in the box. This is important so the pitcher can pitch to the batters weakness. If the batter is deep then the pitcher wants to throw shallow and vice versa.

As far as catching the actual pitch, there is no need for you to catch it in the air. In fact, that could be quite dangerous, especially if you have a batter who is deep in the box. Let the pitch bounce once then catch it. This is easier anyway and do not be afraid to bare hand it if the throw is offline. Since the pitch will decelerate after it bounces, it will be much easier to catch.

You also do not need to squat down like a baseball catcher does which will wreak havoc on your knees etc. It is better to be comfortable, so just one knee on the ground I have found is very comfortable and a kneepad will help you with this as well.

When it comes to the actual throw to home, being positioned correctly and safety should be foremost in your thinking. I have seen catchers in the third base line half way up; this is not the place to be and is insane. Most of us in slow-pitch are out to have fun and are not looking to collide with the catcher, who may have a death wish. Being behind the plate on a throw will not give you a chance to make the play, so right straight out in front of the plate should do nicely and maybe covering the very top of the plate, but blocking it completely you are taking risks which you just don't need to. You want to make the play not take someone out. I know in the heat of the moment things happen, but no one needs a hospital trip, when they have to get up and work the next day.

Last word on the infielders is to note the type of infields you play on. This should dictate the depth at which the infielders play. On dirt, play as deep as you can since the ball is getting through much quicker. On grass, play in more to make sure the throws will get to the bases in time to make the play, because grass will slow the balls down considerably. Artificial turf is like dirt, it is very quick so play deep.

Infield shifts and for that matter outfield too, is something the coach should signal, but in general you will want to put some sort of shift on when pull hitters etc. are up at bat. This will decrease the chances of the batter being able to get a hit and make it easier for the defense to defend.

As far as actually fielding the ball, I will just cover a few basics. Infielders need to start from a glove down position not glove up. Be in the ready position at all times and when the ball is hit to you immediately get the glove in the dirt. More balls are missed trying to do the opposite and bring the glove down after the ball.

Never be afraid to get your body in front of the ball and block it by going down on one knee if you have to. Charge as many balls as you can otherwise they will always play you. This also holds true for the outfielders. Always try and use two hands when fielding the ball. Outfielders it is easier to run in than back. Keep this mind at all times and if you do have one hit over your head turn around and run full bore do not back peddle.

Chapter 15:

Pitch Selection and the miscellaneous

One thing no one can help you with is your own judgment. You could have the best swing in the world, perfect timing and focus, but if you choose to swing at a pitch, which is out of the strike zone, this is on you. So I will not spend too much time here talking about pitch selection, because by now you should know how important it is and what you will do with different pitch locations.

The pitch location wherever it may be, should immediately take you back mentally to your practice off the tee. Because you practiced (hopefully), the contact points of hitting the outside (for hitting to right center), outside and deep (for down the line), middle (for hitting up the middle), middle front (for left center) and inside and inside way out in front (for down the line), you should now be able to duplicate this in the game. They do not change ever unless you move to different parts of the batter's box.

Swinging at a ball out of the strike zone is really a form of a mental error. You know you should not do it, but sometimes you just cannot help yourself. You can reduce the number of times you do this by always practicing swinging at strikes and by now, I am sure you know how the best way to do this. You see after you practice swinging at strikes long enough off the tee; you will eventually get to the point, where you know what swinging at a strike actually feels like.

The level swing has a certain feel to it and after you do it enough, it will become part of your muscle memory. Then when and if you start to swing at a ball out of the strike zone, you will actually feel yourself starting to do the wrong thing. However, now you will be able to easily stop the contact and follow through to check the swing. When you feel yourself lunging at the ball, simply stop your motion and check your swing. If you feel yourself bend the back knee, or drop the back shoulder, stop your motion and check your swing. This works and it works every time it is tried.

Mental errors are those that can be avoided by thinking ahead. Physical errors are those that happen to even the best, so do not get down on those, as they are going to happen, no matter how much you practice. It is the ones where you throw to the wrong base or run when you should not which you need to keep to a minimum. Another example of a mental error is base running errors. These errors in judgment can and do cost the team a rally and another out.

This is one of the only times I am not aggressive in my approach to the game. I have seen so many stupid base running plays that I now preach the conservative approach of base running and of course this is for slow-pitch only. Because slow-pitch is such a hitter's game, then why not give your teammates a chance to hit you in rather than you trying to take an extra base all the time.

Here is another form of mental error, you may not think is, but it hurts the team when it happens. With situational hitting, you have a base runner on third with less than two outs; all you need to do is hit it to the outfield for the runner to tag and to score the run. Even a fly ball will do. Nevertheless, how many times have you seen the hitter ground out to some infielder in this situation.

Working a count is something you need to think about as well. If you are aggressive this should never come into play but if you are not you will always find yourself behind in the count and at the pitchers mercy. I know so many people who would be awesome hitters if they just learned to be more aggressive on the first and second pitch. However, they get two strikes and have to swing at junk. This is an ongoing mental error in my view.

Chapter 16:

Secrets and strategies of the winning coach

Here is some information which will give you an insight into some of the things which have helped me over the years win many tournaments and league championships without even having the benefit of the best team on the field. Good coaching and strategies can make or break a team and in some cases make up for inadequacies a team may have.

Mental Intimidation is something I tried many years ago when I thought it was warranted and it worked like a charm. It will usually only work once though against the same team. There are different forms you can employ. The easy ones are things like having the whole team looking as sharp as possible with matching hats, pants shirts, batting gloves etc. You may not consider this being a form of intimidation but it can be.

I have had many teams tell us we looked good and it made them think we were a serious opponent. Do not overlook this aspect of preparedness. Of course, it helps if you have the team to back it up, but it does pay to look the part of a professional.

The next one is one of those that you only do once to the same team. One year we were in the finals, which were the best of three games. We found ourselves down a game with two to go. With our backs against the wall, we pulled the rabbit out of the hat trick, which in this case was painting our faces with the team colors like in the movie "Braveheart".

It worked even better than expected and we went on to destroy the opposition with a huge offense and defense second to none. The next two games we won by twelve runs and won the championship. To this day, the coach on that team says we took them completely off guard and it mentally took them out of their game. The funny thing was our whole team did not even do it. Only half the team was crazy enough to paint their faces. Nevertheless, it worked and it worked well, because it got us charged up. Emotion and staying up in this game is everything, especially in tournaments.

Another less subtle form of intimidation, but intimidation nonetheless, is something we tried before another playoff game. During warm-ups and throwing the ball around, we made it a point not to say a word to each other. Total silence was the plan and we did it. It sends a message to the other team that something strange is afoot. This one can be used more than once and still work effectively.

Having loud emotional fans with bells and horns and the like is a good thing to have. It does not guarantee victory, but is nice to have the support and it can make a difference. I am sure there are some other things you can think to do, which would affect the other team mentally these are just a few examples.

Next we will discuss doing a line-up and the different variations you can work with to use the talent that you have on your team to the utmost.

Your highest average hitter does not have to lead off all the time, though this is a traditional way of doing things. I will give you an example of a team I coached and played for a few years back.

The team average was .550, not bad, but not 'A' material either. We had one person hitting .700 a few more hitting high .600's a couple low .600's and so on. We had three or four people who hit homeruns and had good power. I lead off our .700 hitter (who just so happened to have homerun power too) then instead of putting a pure homerun hitter in the clean-up spot, I put our second best hitter who also had power. Most teams are going to play your clean-up spot deep anyway, so putting a high average hitter there instead is not a bad idea, because a single can easily turn into a double with the outfield playing deep. You can put another power hitter # five or six.

Here is the thing though; you want most of your high average hitters in the top five in the order. How you mix and match those is not that important, but getting them the most at bats you possibly can is very important. Many times the top of the line up gets an additional at bat over the course of the game. OK now what do you do with a power hitter who hits around .500? I think the #eight spot and eleven or twelve is good if you can play that many players.

If you are lucky enough to have an entire team with high average hitters and three of them have power I would spread the power out to the #4, 8 and 12 spots respectively.

I remember one year our leadoff person who hit .700 also had power, so the opposing teams would play him in, not knowing he had power too. He was not huge either but could hit the ball to any field at will. He broke a record that year for homeruns on our team with fifteen and this league had no fences. We also only played a twenty-two game season. If I had batted him fourth, there is no way his total would have been anywhere near that. I only did this to catch the other team off guard and it worked well.

Therefore, I am saying all of this to say that you do not always have to put people in traditional roles. Putting all your power #3, 4, 5 & 6, can in fact be a waste because the defense is normally going to be playing back for those spots anyway. Putting high average hitters there (if you can) can be a winning strategy that will produce even more hits and runs.

Base coaching is an important part of the game that when done properly can make a big difference in the outcome of the game. If the base coach sends the runner when they should not, the chances of cutting short a rally are very high. Nothing is more frustrating than have just placed a nice hit then being thrown out at a base you should have never been running for to begin with. I have seen teams taken out of more innings this way than just about all other mental errors combined.

The one time I preach non-aggressiveness is when it comes to base running. This is especially true in slow-pitch where everyone in the line-up can get an easy base hit, so do yourself and the team a favor and let them do just that.

Base coaches need to know your talent and speed of the runner and base runners need to listen to the coaches plain and simple.

Keeping the players happy as much as possible is important for team chemistry but not always possible. You may have a few problem personalities on the team such as poor sportsmen and the like which can make both playing and coaching not as enjoyable as it could be. In a perfect world, there never would be players who lose their temper etc. but on real teams, this is something the coach has to deal with before things get out of hand.

If you let it fester, it will get worse, so the proper thing to do is to try to nip it in the bud. In some cases, suspending the offending player may be the only remedy. A verbal warning is OK for a while, but suspensions work much better and yes, this is the coach's responsibility. Do not leave it for the umpires or league director to have to tell you how to get control of your team.

In severe cases, it is better to have an offending player booted for the entire season, rather than having the whole season ruined for the entire team. The players will respect you much more if you take care of problems before they get uncontrollable.

Ok on to some more pleasant tasks. If you have a bench full of players for example let's say you have fifteen people to get into a single game, there are a few ways to do it. Many players would rather play half a game then sit an entire one, so if you can get as many players involved as you can. Players sitting the bench can coach bases etc. Whoever sat the game before should play a full game the next time around and so on.

Substitutions can be made, so everyone gets an equal amount of playing time throughout the season. This of course is if you want to be fair. Come playoff time you may want to change this, but whatever you do, you want to have an understanding with the players as to what your strategy is and what their role may be.

Many years ago, we were having many problems with forfeits on many teams in the league, so we instituted a new rule that virtually eliminated forfeits altogether. We simply came up with a twelve-player rule that allowed more people to get into the game.

We previously had eleven with one player being a designated hitter. This was ok, but adding a twelfth made all the difference. The Extra player or extra hitter as we call it gives the coach the option of having two designated hitters and thus keeps more people interested and showing up to the games week after week. You still can play just ten if you want but twelve is the maximum and you should think about bringing this up at your next league meeting if your league has problems with forfeits.

Coaching kids is much more rewarding than adults in my opinion. Its fun to watch the little ones do the things that will some day form the basis of solid play. It is also nice to see them improve week in and out and have fun while they do it. Coach's need to try to keep it fun at the young ages and teach them that it is not just about winning that is important, but how they play the game and their attitudes are more important than winning.

This does not mean you do not keep score and do not reward the winners, but it should not be the all out focus at the beginning stages. Watching kids win a championship is a great feeling too, but the other team played hard to get there as well and should be given credit, where credit is due.

As far as instruction goes, keeping it simple is better with kids. Most kids will not be able to watch an instructional video of any length and get a whole lot out of it. You as a coach or parent should watch them yourself and then break down the information, to teach them one basic at a time to build on it until they can comprehend more later on.

Chapter 17: Final thoughts

The last thing you need to know is, no matter what technique or system you choose to employ for yourself, (hopefully it is mine), but you will at times still not be successful as you know you can be. This is simply because of a lack of mental focus. This one thing sets the pros apart from the masses. They have learned how to focus longer and harder than the rest of us. Even they occasionally have mental lapses, which are apparent at times, and they have the best systems and methods in the world.

So do not get down on yourself, or more importantly the technique or system you are using when things to go as planned. It is not the systems fault, just like it's not faulty equipment or the bat. It never is. There is inevitably going to be at bats or maybe even games where for whatever reason your focus and eye contact are lacking. However, your times of non-focus will be shorter if you have a system to follow rather than shooting in the dark. In addition, the system will help you in those times of non-focus just as it helps me. The following things you need to do, to become the best hitter you can be and stay there.

1. View the video and review as many times as you can to commit the timing technique to memory.

2. Practice what you have viewed and read, until you become comfortable with it (there is no substitute for practice) never is, never will be.

3. Employ the technique on each pitch whether ball or strike.

4. Constantly remind yourself to keep focus and eye contact on the ball, because this is where everyone (even the pros) loses it every now and again.

5. Always come back to review the basics both in the book and the video. Over time, you will forget certain things you have learned, so you will constantly need to refresh and go back to the basics.

6. Do yourself a huge favor and go get a good batting tee and use it at least once a week or more if possible. You have to get a tee!

Optional: Watch and listen to your teammates and opponents marvel at your newfound talent that was simply lying in wait. Then tell them (if you feel like it), as to how you changed your game!

Remember this too, no matter what you do and even when you feel like you are doing everything right, it is still a game of adjustments. Sometimes things temporarily go wrong for me, that's when I realize I need to make slight adjustments to what I am doing to make it happen for me again. A great example of this is when you get to be a truly great hitter and it won't take long, word gets out and then you will see fewer and fewer strikes to hit. At that point you will need to be even more patient and check those swings and or in many cases just take the walk.

No one likes to walk, but if they are not going to give you a pitch to hit, it may be your only option. Another adjustment you may need to make is if you are far away from the plate, like I sometimes like to be, the pitcher may try and throw farther and farther outside never giving you a pitch over the plate let alone an inside pitch. Well this is fine for opposite field hitting, but if you want to hit up the middle or pull it's not going to happen, so simply move closer to the plate and you will be hitting up the middle again and pulling more.

Also make sure you don't hesitate after you start your motion to swing. It needs to be one smooth motion back to come forward with hands back as far as possible, never hesitating at any point. As long as you are doing a head count this should not happen, but if you are contacting the ball too late then you are most likely hesitating at some point. Work it out on the tee and you will see what I mean.

I leave you with this final example: The example is me. Yes, I am the person who came up with the perfect Timing technique for slo-pitch and it is awesome when it is put to use. But guess what even I, the guy that knows how to be the best hitter you can be and help others achieve their hitting best, doesn't always follow his own system.

How can this be? I attribute it to mental lapses, laziness and trying different things and gizmos that do not work. This is the only thing I can attribute it. I do not always do what I am supposed to do, even when I know exactly what the right thing is! In addition, I am not successful when I do not follow my own system that I formulated.

The reason there are coaches in the major leagues is because players need to be reminded constantly what the right thing is along with making slight adjustments. You see even they occasionally forget the basics and start bad habits that need to be broken.

Thanks for reading my book and viewing my video. Now go and get good, but most importantly have fun. Who knows some day you might even go pro!

** I dedicate this project to you the player, my family for their patience and love, my friends and teammates and most importantly to Jesus Christ my personal Savior. Without him first, none of this would have been possible. Enjoy what he has given me to give you.

45709140R00082

Made in the USA
Lexington, KY
06 October 2015